"MAN'S BEST FRIEND"

(But The Entire City Loves Him)
VOLUME II

"Solidarity of Alofus & Lieutenant Dooley On The Horizon"
2014

By

JOHN A. GREER SR.

(New Author)

President and CEO of Baskart International Inc.,
Poe Pemps Inc., Allen's International Inc. (A.I.)
325 Hwy 80 E. Suite 106 Clinton, Ms 39056

Creating
Books that will inspire all ages to believe that they can achieve.

"MAN'S BEST FRIEND"
(But the Entire City Loves Him)
ALOFUS-synonymous to <u>All of Us.</u>

To explain how Alofus came about and acquainted with the Dooley Family is that a while back the Dooley Family got a visit from NaNa and Paw Paw--the grandparents of Little Jay and Diamerald Alexus, NaNa and Paw Paw had a dog named Missy, Missy was a female Australian Shepherd who was pregnant. Shortly thereafter Missy went into labor prematurely, and gave birth to six puppies, but unfortunately due to medical conditions five of the six puppies died within a twenty four hour period. So NaNa and Paw Paw were determined to save the last puppy, they took this last puppy to the vet and he was put on life support in an incubator. While on life support NaNa and Paw Paw got lots of support from all over the city the puppy gained lots of popularity and fame for his determination to live, everyone prayed for the puppy and donated money to help on the expenses to try and save him. Then after about six weeks past the doctor of the veterinarian hospital gave a thumbs up that the puppy was okay now, and that he would survive on its own. Almost everyone in the city was thrilled but for a few individuals who thought it was absurd for the city to put that much emphasis on an animal. Nevertheless NaNa and Paw Paw never gave up, and Missy was also thrilled to still have one of her puppies survive. She showed it by almost licking him to death as the camera's from the media captured that special moment. Now almost two months had passed, NaNa and Paw Paw had gotten so caught up in trying to save Missy's last puppy that they almost had forgotten about there grandson Little Jay who had a birth day coming up on the next day., so NaNa Paw Paw and Missy got in their car and drove across town to take the surviving puppy to their grandson for his birthday--because that's all he used to talk about is that when Missy have her puppies that he surely wanted one, and after the puppy had fully grown, that he wanted for himself, his dad and Paw Paw to all go hunting together. Now, it was time for NaNa, Paw Paw and Missy to return home it was getting late and it had begun to rain as well., so they all got into the car and drove home, unfortunately they didn't make it back home. They were all killed in a car wreck when Paw Paw lost control of the vehicle due to a strange obstacle running across in front of the car, and it went over an embankment. So now here we are the day of the funeral at the home of the Dooley Family--sadden for their lost all sitting around in the family room after the funeral gathered together, and dad speaks saying, how about we all decide on a name for the new family addition.

Created By,

John A.Greer Sr.

LITTLE ALOFUS

Man's Best Friend

"But the Entire City Loves Him"
Volume II

"Solidarity of Alofus & Lieutenant Dooley On The Horizon"
2014

JOHN A. GREER SR.

Order this book online at www.trafford.com
or email orders@trafford.com

Most Trafford titles are also available at major online book retailers.

Printed in the United States of America.

ISBN: 978-1-4669-0166-7 (sc)
ISBN: 978-1-4669-0167-4 (hc)
ISBN: 978-1-4669-0153-7 (e)

Library of Congress Control Number: 2011918962

Trafford rev. 03/03/2014

 www.trafford.com

North America & International
toll-free: 1 888 232 4444 (USA & Canada)
fax: 812 355 4082

The
Things that an individual will learn from reading this book, though it
is fictional, is that
if we work together for the common good of humanity and
Man's Best Friend,
we can defeat anything that might get in the way.

What this book will attempt to prove is that when an individual
(or an Entire City) has love and perseverance, they have hope and
strength.

This book is dedicated to
Everyone who has Man's Best Friend
As a companion,
People who love Dogs
And moreover, humankind as we now know it.

CRITIQUE
This thrill-filled novel has an eloquent nature, and is so
entertaining,that the entire family will enjoy it...
Because of Alofus' and the other main characters' likeable
personalities,
the readers will find themselves falling in love with this book, thus
making it somewhat of a love story...

Reading comprised of
D-SCARF
Drama--that is delineative and realistic,
Suspense--that will keep you guessing and on your toes,
Comedy--that is sporadic,
Action--that readers will anticipate seeing on the big screen,
Romance--that is unadulterated, and
Friendship- that exemplifies loyalty and unity among the family
(Stay tuned for future books to come with the D-SCARF syndrome
in mind.)

Cast of Characters in the Story

1. <u>Alofus</u>: Little Jay's dog
2. <u>Little Jay</u>: Jonathan Dooley, Jr.
3. <u>Mr. Dooley</u>: Jonathan Dooley, Sr- A Policeman.
4. <u>NaNa</u>: Little Jay's grandma
5. <u>Paw Paw</u>: Little Jay's grandpa
6. <u>Missy</u>: NaNa and Paw Paw's dog
7. <u>Mrs. Dooley</u>: Lillian Dooley
8. <u>Diamerald Alexus</u>: Little Jay's sister
9. <u>Jimmy</u>: June Bug- Bully #1
10. <u>Robi</u>: Bully #2.
11. <u>Mr. Giradeli</u>: Robi's dad
12. <u>Ms. Nuttingham</u>: Jimmy's grandma
13. <u>Nappy Headed Squirrel</u>: Kenny (young man) - Associate of June Bug
14. <u>Guy at Counter</u>: Works at the pool hall
15. <u>Manager</u>: Manages the pool hall
16. <u>Guy in Vehicle</u>: Informant who flags Mr. Dooley down ouside of the pool hall
17. <u>Money Mike</u>: Alfred Kincade- Mr. Dooley's nemesis
18. <u>Serg. Willansby</u>: Friend and ex girlfriend of Mr. Dooley
19. <u>Dr. Elenski</u>: Former professor at the university- Creator of M&M's Pool Hall
20. <u>Dr. Satcher</u>: Former president of the college board
21. <u>Dr. Olgaston</u>: Director of personnel at JSU
22. <u>Professor Greer</u> : Present director over the lab- Former co worker and assistant of Dr. Elenski
23. <u>Hanna</u>: Diamerald's room mate
24. <u>Chief McClemens</u>: Chief of Police Dept.
25. <u>Barbara</u>: Serg. Willansby's daughter
26. <u>Kellie</u>: Mrs. Dooley's sister
27. <u>Mark</u>: Kellie's son
28. <u>Officer Bradley</u>: Ofc. That calls Mr. Dooley about Alofus
29. <u>Officer Lansing</u>: Ofc. who found Alofus injured.
30. <u>Corporal Davenport</u>: Ofc.ordered to move crowd back at crime scene

31. <u>Serg. Ortega</u>: Ofc.with crime scene unit
32. <u>Dr. Smortzen</u>: Veterinarian- Dr. at M.A.V.A.S.H.
33. <u>Dr. Kyzar</u>: Professor Greer's colleague
34. <u>Corporal Becker</u>: Ofc. who calls Mr. Dooley about Serg. Willansby's whereabouts
35. <u>Captain Valezquez</u>: Swat team commander
36. <u>Dr. Latrell</u>: Dr. at St. Mary's Hospital
37. <u>Dr. Chivonotsky</u>: Forensic specialist at crime lab

WHY I WROTE THIS BOOK

I have yet to meet a human being that has the best of every physical attribute- beauty, brawn, and brilliance. Whenever we strive to have something a certain way, better than it already is, we are by definition, fighting a losing battle. Rather than being thankful and content with the card life dealt us, we as a people, focus on what's wrong with our bodies and our need to change it. Sad yet true, zeroing in on our defects implies that we are dissatisfied with ourselves... For what?... Carrying a few extra, undesirable pounds? Not running as fast as some other people? Not being as strong as some other people? Looking older than people who are actually older than us? The very act of focusing on these imperfections distracts us from the real reason God created us, which is to love one another, no matter the features. Don't get me wrong, the body is God's temple and he wants us to maintain it. However, even though there's always room for improvement, we should be careful not to become obsessed by putting too much emphasis on our looks. Remember... everything God created was good... very good. Therefore, we should enjoy and appreciate who we are. And besides, as we have borne the image of the earthy, we shall also bear the image of the heavenly. For this corruptible must put on incorruption, and this mortal must put on immortality. In a world where judgment is absent, every**body** is good. So in closing, this is why I decided to create such a book, to help enlighten the readers about the dangers of tampering with God's creations... mankind and man's best friend.

Acknowledgments

I would like to acknowledge the following for inspiring and assisting me in the creation of this second book Volume II. First and foremost, I thank God almighty and His son, Jesus Christ, for affording me the wisdom and enginuity to continue the story that He inspired me to create and for impressing upon my mind of heart to continue such a story. It was meant to be a fictive narrative but I call it my F.A.T. book (Fiction Approximating Truth) because it does, somewhat, sing of my own personal life, thus creating (I guess you could say) a half-truth narrative.

I'd also like to thank my mom, Mary Greer Watson, who was called home to glory on February 20, 2008. To her husband and my step-father Robert Watson who passed away in 2008. Also a younger brother of mine by the name of Jeffery who was killed in a car wreck in 1993. Wilce (Buddy) Day a military veteran and uncle of mine who was like a father to me, who also passed away in 2009, and to his lovely and devoted wife Mary Ellen, who preceded him in death in 2008. Also I would like to recognize another military veteran as well as a dear and loyal uncle of mine who passed away in 2011 a Mr. Otis Washington Sr. We're going to miss you unc. May you rest in peace. To you all who afforded me with the necessary attributes to be the man that I have become. I'll always remember and love you. Thank you also, Lord Jesus, for such a devoted help mate and friend, the one and only Valerie my wife, along with our wonderful supporting cast of children, Tracy, Jacelyn, John Jr., Shawn, Jeffrey, and Alexis. And our grandchildren Destiny, Trerell, Johannah, Janeece, Latrell. Also there are two other interesting individuals in my life that I could dare not make mention, my dear aunt and second mom, Pearline Johnson. For by her awesome and unchanging faith, she inspires me to continue to trust in the Lord. I'll never forget you my dear sweet clementine. And to a very special true friend and mom figure of mine who passed away in 1990. My dear sweet mother-in-law Lillie Johnson, better known as (Sweet Lillie). We love you and miss your company. I also would like to extend my most humble thanks, gratitude and support from all of my surviving siblings James, Melvin, Barbara, Sharon, Patricia, Archie, Brenda, and Eric, along with a host of beautiful and wonderful nieces, nephews, Aunts, Uncles,Cousins and Friends. And to each and every one of the wonderful supporters of my first book Volume I. Entitled "Man's Best Friend" (But The Entire City Loves Him) Thanks. For without God's guidance and his devine inspiration and to all who helped me to bring this second book into fruition, Volume II.of "Man's Best Friend" (But The Entire City Loves Him) Entitled "The Solidarity Of Alofus And Lieutenant Dooley On The Horizon.Without you all I could not have done it. Love you Guys.

John A. Greer Sr.
My Contact Info: E-MAIL ADDRESS (Jaguar 1959@gmail.Com)
325 Hwy 80East Clinton, Miss. 39056

(Last time, Mr. Dooley had just finished talking to Dr. Chivonotsky about some possible evidence that had been found, a couple of shoe imprints. However, that work is an ongoing process. Meanwhile, Mr. Dooley is on the phone with his wife, informing her that he is on his way home.)

Mrs. Dooley: Hello? . . . Hi there, sweetheart. Boy, am I glad to hear from you!

Mr. Dooley: I knew it all alone honey, that I am to irresistible for you to stay mad at me.

Mrs. Dooley: Well, not to burst your bubble darling, but as irresistible as you might thank that you are, that is not the reason I'm glad to hear from you.

Mr. Dooley: It isn't? Then why else are you glad to hear from me?

Mrs. Dooley: Okay, if you insist on knowing Mr. Irresistable, the real reason I'm glad to hear from you is because, with all that has gone on here lately. I was afraid that you might've been kidnapped or something.

Mr. Dooley: Me?! kidnapped?! Now who would want to kidnap a broke, middle aged black man?

Mrs. Dooley: Who?! Oh I guess you must have forgotten something darling? I would suspect the same people who kidnapped your broke, middle aged black female partner, and not to mention our dog too, that's who.

1

Mr. Dooley: Alright now honey, it's not fair for you to be making a mockery of Sergeant Willansby's abduction. Especially under these circumstances.

Mrs. Dooley: Well excuse me? Am I missing something here? Because it seems to me that you're getting a little to testy over your partner in crime, wouldn't you say?

Mr. Dooley: Missing something?! Just what does that suppose to mean, honey?

Mrs. Dooley: What it means, "Mr. Willansby wanna be". Is why on earth are you defending Sergeant Willansby, instead of Little Jay's dog, Alofus? Could it be, because you spent more time with her than, with Little Jay and Alofus.

Mr. Dooley: Now why would you say something like that, sweetheart? Where is all this coming from?

Mrs. Dooley: Let's just say that even though I'm just a pharmacist, as opposed to being a high profile detective like yourself, I too am capable of solving cases.

Mr. Dooley: Solving cases?! Should I dare not ask you, Renee, what thats suppose to mean? (Renee being Mrs. Dooley's middle name).

Mrs. Dooley: Oh, so I'm Renee now? Now I know you're guilty. Because the only time you ever call me Renee, is when you've done something wrong and are looking for a way out.

Mr. Dooley: Okay, enough already; I've had a very hard day and the last thing I need right now is to be arguing with you about something as frivolous as this.

Mrs. Dooley: I know you didn't just say that this conversation was frivolous . . . Okay, "Mr. Valuator", I guess I'll just have to show you how frivolous this conversation is.

Mr. Dooley: No, Honey; I didn't say that this conversation was frivolous, I said that the arguing was, and I meant that.

Mrs. Dooley: Alright then and I mean this. You can quit with the honey crap, because at this point, it doesn't matter how you phrase it. I'm through with this discussion . . . Oh, and by the way, don't you have to get back to the hospital and check up on your partner? (Then Mrs. Dooley hangs up the phone in Mr. Dooley's face).

Mr. Dooley: Now what are . . . Hello? Hello? Honey, are you there?

(Now Mr. Dooley is very upset, so he decides to take a detour and go to his getaway to cool off, because he feels that going home while he and Mrs. Dooley are upset would possibly create a bigger problem between them. While en route to Poe Pemp's lounge,

Mr. Dooley decides to give Ms. Nuttingham {Little Jimmy's grandma} a call. He hasn't spoken to her since he dropped Little Jimmy back off at home and he wants to check up on Jimmy's behavior. Ms. Nuttingham is now answering the phone . . .)

Ms. Nuttingham: Now I done told you, you ole nappy headed, good fa nuth . . . (Ms. Nuttingham is interrupted by Mr. Dooley.)

Mr. Dooley: Ms. Nuttingham . . . Ms. Nuttingham, hold on; this is Lieutenant Dooley.

Ms. Nuttingham: Who you say dis is?

Mr. Dooley: I'm Lieutenant Dooley, ma'am; the police officer who brought Little Jimmy back to your house a few days ago, remember?

Ms. Nuttingham: Oh yeah! I remember now; you dat cop dat help me with my June Bug.

Mr. Dooley: Yes ma'am, that's right, and my name is Lieutenant Dooley. Is everything okay, Ms. Nuttingham? Were you expecting someone else?

Ms. Nuttingham: I'm sorry Mista, I thought you wuz dat ole nappy headed squirrel. He been callin' here fa June Bug all day long. I told him dat June Bug ain't here but he keeps-a-callin' anyway, so I keeps-a-hangin' up on him.

Mr. Dooley: What do you mean, June Bug's not there? Why isn't he there, Ms. Nuttingham?

Ms. Nuttingham: I reckon he ain't here 'cause he done went back to dat ole hole in the wall where'z he loves to hang out.

Mr. Dooley: Are you sure that it's Squirrel who keeps calling you, and are you sure that Jimmy has gone back to the pool hall?

Ms. Nuttingham: Well son, like they say, ain't nuthin' sho but death and taxes, so I can't say dat my June Bug is back at dat place fa sho, but one thang I do know fa sho is dat da calls I keep—a gettin' are from dat nappy headed squirrel.

Mr. Dooley: How are you so sure about that, Ms. Nuttingham?

Ms. Nuttingham: 'Cause June Bug got me dis new phone dat showz me folks' names befo I ansa.

Mr. Dooley: Yes, I understand now, Ms. Nuttingham. What you're saying is that you have caller I.D.

Ms. Nuttingham: Calla what? I don't know what they callz it, but what-so-neva it tiz, I can see da numba.

Mr. Dooley: Then why did you think I was Squirrel, Ms. Nuttingham? Is it because you can't see too well?

Ms. Nuttingham: Nah, dat ain't it, 'cause I gotz my glasses on and I can see just fine wit e'm.

(Now Mr. Dooley understands how Ms. Nuttingham got his identity confused with Squirrel's. He believes that Ms. Nuttingham can read numbers but can't read words, and it's possible that his and Squirrel's phone numbers are similar. Nevertheless, he now wants to refocus his attention on locating Jimmy, so he decides to see if Ms. Nuttingham can get him Squirrel's number . . .)

Mr. Dooley: Ms. Nuttingham, I was wondering if you could get Squirrel's number from the front of the phone and give it to me.

Ms. Nuttingham: Sho can, Mista, only I don't have to get it off the phone 'cause it's right here on the frigerata. June Bug put it there fa me so'z I could call e'm iffen I needed e'm.

Mr. Dooley: Well now, that was rather smart and nice of Jimmy; you see there's hope for him after all. Now can you please read the number to me, ma'am?

Ms. Nuttingham: I sho can. Are you ready?

Mr. Dooley: Yes ma'am, I'm ready.

Ms. Nuttingham: Ah-ite, da first numba is a seven and the next numba is a two, afta dat is a five, then a dash and a four, then a three, a six and anuda six. Now do you have it, or do I have to say it agen?

Mr. Dooley: No ma'am, you don't have to say it again. You did well; thank you, and Ms. Nuttingham . . .

Ms. Nuttingham: Yeah, what is it now, Mista?

Mr. Dooley: Oh, it's nothing, I just wanted to let you know that I'm about to call that Squirrel guy and see if he knows where Jimmy is.

Ms. Nuttingham: Okay, dat's good, and you be sho to call me back and let me know iffen you find out somethin', okay Mista?

Mr. Dooley: Yes ma'am, I will be sure to do that. Goodbye.

(They both hang up. Then Mr. Dooley dials Squirrel's number, which is very similar to his, being that his number is 752-4366 and Squirrel's is 725-4366. Squirrel is now answering his phone . . .)

Squirrel: Yeah, what up? Dis ya boy Squirrel in dis messed up world, I.m probably out tryna make a dolla so go ahead and holla. Leave a message at the tone and I'll call you later on. (The phone beeps. Mr. Dooley realizes that he has gotten Squirrel's voice mail. He decides to go ahead and leave a message, hoping that Squirrel will soon return his call.)

Mr. Dooley: Hello Squirrel, this is Lieutenant Dooley of the Jackson Police Department. I hope you recognize me by now. Anyway, if it's not asking too much of your precious time, I'd like for you to give me a call ASAP; in other words, as soon as you get this message. It's about Little Jimmy; he's missing again. I'm wondering if he's there or if you might know his whereabouts. If not, thanks anyway, Squirrel. My number is 752-4366; that should be easy to remember since it's very similar to your number. I'm waiting on your call so get back to me.

(Mr. Dooley hangs up. He's now in front of Poe Pemp's lounge. He exits his vehicle and heads inside, where he finds Captain Valezquez {of SWAT} drinking at the bar. Captain Valezquez recognizes Mr. Dooley and invites him to join him at the bar . . .)

Capt. Valezquez: Why, hello there, Lieutenant Dooley! What's going on?

Mr. Dooley: Hello to you, Captain Valezquez. Nothing's going on except the same ole stuff.

Capt. Valezquez: Yeah, I feel you on that one, Lieutenant. What are you having? I'm buying.

Mr. Dooley: Oh, I got it, Captain, but thanks anyhow.

Capt. Valezquez: No, no, allow me; it's an honor sir. Please sit down. There's something I need to discuss with you anyway. Now what'll you have?

Mr. Dooley: Alright then, since you insist, I'll have a whiskey sour on the rocks.

(Captain Valezquez beckons for the bartender to come over.)

Capt. Valezquez: (talking to bartender) Pour the lieutenant a whiskey sour on the rocks please, and give me another round of G and J.

(After they receive their drinks, Mr. Dooley speaks . . .)

Mr. Dooley: Thanks, Captain Valezquez. Now what is it that you wanted to discuss with me?

Capt. Valezquez: Well Lieutnant, I'm not going to beat around the bush, because I feel that you need to know this. As I said earlier, we good cops, though we be few in numbers, have to stick together. After all, David did slay Goliath, didn't he?

Mr. Dooley: Alright, Captain Valezquez, I don't mean to be rude but I'm not in the mood for riddles right now. I don't have much time to waste, so if you got something to say, please come on out with it.

Capt. Valezquez: Okay, okay, Lieutenant; just chill out a minute. Take a sip of your drink, and I'll fill you in on the latest scoop, ah-ite?

Mr. Dooley: Whatever, man. I'm sorry, okay? I guess I do need a drink. (He sips his drink. As he sets it back down, he gets a call. He looks at his phone and sees Squirrel's number, so he ask Captain Valezquez to excuse him while he answers.) Hello? Lieutenant Dooley here.

Squirrel: Yeah, Lieutenant Dooley, what's up, my nigga? How can a brother be of service?

Mr. Dooley: Did you just call me a nigga and your brother in the same breath?

Squirrel: Yes, I did. Why? Do you got a problem with that too, Lieutenant Dooley?

Mr. Dooley: Why would you want a nigga to be your brother, Squirrel? Wouldn't you rather have someone that you can trust to be your brother?

Squirrel: Man, you know what I'm talking about; you know it's only slang. Do you always take things literally, Lieutenant Dooley?

Mr. Dooley: No, because if I did, I wouldn't be talking to you, because the only squirrels that talk are the cartoons, Alvin and the chipmonks, and Rocky on the Bullwinkle show .

Squirrel: Ah-ite, now that was a good one; I guess left myself open for that one. Only thing I know who Alvin and the chipmonks are; but who the heck is Rocky on the bullwinkle show?

Mr. Dooley: Oh my bad, you're to young I forgot that was before your time. Although Alvin and the chipmonks were too, but they did a remake for you guys. Anyhow Rocky was a flying squirrel in cartoon town okay.

Squirrel: Cool, that sounds like it was awesome, I wish they would do a remake of that character.

Mr. Dooley: They did it was called, ole nappy headed flying squirrrel, but it was a flop.

(Squirrel begins to laugh because he knows that Mr. Dooley is referring to himself.)

Squirrel: You know what, man, ain't nobody made me laugh that hard in a while, not even Ms. Nuttingham herself. You feel me?

Mr. Dooley: Yeah, I feel you, my nigga.

Squirrel: Oh, so you got jokes now?

Mr. Dooley: No Squirrel, it's no joke. I'm hoping that you are really my nigga, and that you are now ready to give me the 411 on Little Jimmy.

Squirrel: Oh yeah, I forgot! I called you back because of that voice mail you left me, but I ain't seen June Bug, Mr. Dooley, on the real this time. I've been calling his house because I wanted to talk to him myself, but every time I called, that crazy old ha . . .

(Squirrel is interrupted by Mr. Dooley.)

Mr. Dooley: Hold on there, Squirrel! I'm sorry but I won't allow you to disrespect Ms. Nuttiingham. She's nearly four times your age and besides, didn't your parents teach you to respect your elders, son?

Squirrel: Yeah, you're right, Lieutenant Dooley; my bad . . . but as for my parents, no, they didn't teach me anything. They just brought me here and then deserted me like a lot of other parents have done to their kids. You know what I'm saying?

Mr. Dooley: No son, not exactly. What are you saying, Squirrel?

Squirrel: Well, my parents had me and then gave me up for adoption, and Jimmy was also left behind by his parents, who I think got a divorce or somehing. I know a lot of other kids who were ditched, too; that's what I'm saying, Lieutenant.

Mr. Dooley: First off, Squirrel, I'm sorry to hear about your parents giving you up for adoption. I didn't know, and I don't know how that feels either but I'm pretty sure it doesn't feel good. As for Jimmy's parents divorcing each other, my understanding was that they were still together, but his dad ended up in jail after killing his mom for messing around and leaving with another guy, which is why Ms. Nuttingham had to raise Jimmy. So you see, Squirrel, it's not exactly the same situation as your parents giving you away.

Squirrel: It ain't, huh? Well, he doesn't have any parents and neither do I, so what's the difference, Lieutenant Dooley?

Mr. Dooley: Well, for one, Jimmy did get to know his parents, though briefly. That's why it has had a more profound effect on him, because he knows what he's missing . . . unlike yourself, Squirrel. You never got to know anything about your parents, and I'm almost certain that, that had a great impact on your life and decision making.

Squirrel: (yelling) How would you know, Lieutenant?! You've probably had it good all your life. What would you know about how Jimmy or I feel?

Mr. Dooley: Honestly, Squirrel, I don't know how it feels from you or Little Jimmy's perspectives . . . but I know someone who does and he's speaking through me right now, telling you that he feels you and Little Jimmy's pain, and he doesn't want you all to carry that burden any longer. That's why he died on Calvary, so that people like you and Little Jimmy could be free of all the hurt, pain, and neglect. He died for everyone who would believe and receive him into their hearts. He died for, not only your sins, but for all who wanted to be saved from this untoward generation. You see, Squirrel, he picked up the cross and suffered so that we wouldn't have to. All you have to do right now, son, is confess that Jesus Christ is your Savior and believe it in your heart.

Squirrel: I hear everything you're saying, Lieutenant Dooley, and I've heard that crap all my life, but I still feel all the pain myself, so don't give me that baloney.

Mr. Dooley: You know what, son? I know that you still feel pain and hurt . . . but do you know why?

Squirrel: Let me guess, because I don't believe, right?

Mr. Dooley: No, that's not right. Squirrel, the bible teaches us that a man that is born of a woman is of a few days and is full of trouble, but God said that if we put our trust in Him, the devil in hell can't touch us, unless of course, God allows him to and sometimes God will do just that, but only to test our faith. You see, Squirrel, God is the potter and we're the clay. He created us in His own image and He wants us to trust that He will keep us. Moreover, God wants us to believe that He is able to do above and beyond all that we ask of Him. And when one's mother and father leaves them, God says that he will be there to pick them up. Also, If our ways please Him, He will even give us the desires of our hearts; now that's saying a lot, son. However, we seem to think that it takes a lot to please Him and it doesn't. Sometimes we try to please men rather than God, and that's where we fail . . . Anyhow, I didn't mean to preach to you, but I am a vessel of God's and He can use me anytime He wants. The seed is now planted within you,

Squirrel, and from here on out, it's up to you to cultivate that seed so that it may grow. Just keep holding on to the faith. God loves you, son and so do I . . . And remember this, the best person that anyone could have as their parent is the Lord and Savior, Jesus Christ. I've gotta go now. I'll be praying with you, Squirrel. Meanwhile, will you promise to give me a call if you hear anything about Jimmy?

Squirrel: Yes sir, I will be more than happy to do that; not just for you, Lieutenant Dooley, but for Jimmy and Ms. Nuttingham as well . . . And thanks for talking with me and taking account of my feelings.

Mr. Dooley: Squirrel, you know that you're welcome, but we weren't just talking; we were feasting together in the word. In other words, Squirrel, we were praying . . . and the bible teaches us that where two or three are gathered together in God's name, touching and agreeing, there He will be in the midst, so guess what Squirrel . . .

Squirrel: What, Lieutenant Dooley?

Mr. Dooley: There was a third person on the line with you and me . . . and that's why everything's gonna be alright. Even though we have confusion in this world, in God we have peace. Goodbye Squirrel. (Squirrel says goodbye, and they both hang up. Captain Valezquez is now sitting with his mouth agape. For he overheard Mr. Dooley's message to Squirrel and is in awe of it.)

Capt. Valezquez: Man, that was a good sermon! You know what, Lieutenant Dooley? I've been going to church at least . . . (starts counting with his fingers) . . . three to four times a year, and I ain't never heard a message with such power in it. Can you come over my house and talk to my two kids, Lieutenant Dooley? I have a boy and a girl, both teenagers, and sometimes

I don't know what to say to them. (Mr. Dooley and Captain Valezquez both laugh.)

Mr. Dooley: Thanks for the compliment, Captain but, all jokes aside, that wasn't me, so I can't take the credit.

Capt. Valezquez: Then how do I get hold of that fella that just finished talking?

Mr. Dooley: Just dial 53787, then push the send button; and I promise he will answer.

Capt. Valezquez: What are you talking about, Lieutenant?

Mr. Dooley: Just look at those numbers on your cell phone, Captain Valezquez, and the letters above them. What do they spell?

Capt. Valezquez: Oh wow; you're a wiz, man! How did you do that? Do you know that those letters spell "JESUS"?

Mr. Dooley: No, Captain Valezquez. Actually, I thought they spelled "KERUP" . . . you know, like "corrupt" . . . until Jesus showed me that I could turn the KERUP into love, because God is love and He and Jesus are one in the same. Are you feeling me here, Captain?

Capt. Valezquez: Yeah, "Brother Dooley", I'm feeling you; preach on. (They both laugh again.)

Mr. Dooley: Alright, let's settle back down to the real world. What did you want to discuss with me, Captain Valezquez?

Capt. Valezquez: Well sir, to be straightforward, I have an aquaintance who is an FBI agent; and the word is, your chief and a few others in the department are under investigation. Now before I go any further, I must stress the importance of your secretion, Lieutenant. You can't mention this to a soul; not your sergeant, not your wife . . . you can't even dial the 53787 number and tell him.

Mr. Dooley: Let's not get crazy here, okay Captain? You and I both know that whatever it is, he already knows.

Capt. Valezquez: I know, I know; I'm just kidding, but it really is just that serious, Lieutenant.

Mr. Dooley: I understand the severity of this matter, and I wouldn't dare let it leak and endanger someone.

Capt. Valezquez: Good, because that someone could be you, my aquaintance, or even myself, but since I see that you understand, here it goes . . . The word is that your chief is in cahoots with a Dr. Elenski, money laundering and working on some strange, scientific experiment.

Mr. Dooley: Not to bust you or your brilliant FBI friends' bubbles, Captain Valezquez, but I've already concluded that in the few days that I've been working the Satcher case.

Capt. Valezquez: Good for you, "Lieutenant Smart Aleck", but that's not the icing on the cake; that's only the batter being mixed. And when all is said and the mixing is done, the icing is ready to spread, Lieutenant. Guest what? The Mayor is the icing on the cake, if you get my drift.

(Mr. Dooley is very surprised, but not totally shocked, because the Mayor is Chief McClemens' stepfather.)

Mr. Dooley: Now that explains quite a few things.

Capt. Valezquez: Things like what, Lieutenant Dooley?

Mr. Dooley: Well, for one, it explains why the chief would want to surpress evidence against Dr. Elenski.

Capt. Valezquez: What?! Now you can't be serious.

Mr. Dooley: Yes, I am, Captain. Why else would the FEDS be involved?

Capt. Valezquez: Yeah, I guess you're right, but I thought it was only for the money laundering. I honestly thought that Chief McClemens was a victim of circumstance, because of his relationship to Mayor Adovis.

Mr. Dooley: What do you mean by that?

Capt. Valezquez: What I mean is that our Mayor is a more likely candidate for money laundering, especially since he has his own private jet and a couple of luxurious getaway homes; one down in the Florida Keys and another in the Bahamas.

Mr. Dooley: Yeah, you might have a point, Captain Valezquez. After all, Mayor Adovis does have a rather extravagant lifestyle, considering his salary. I just thought he was able to purchase the homes and the jet because he had married Marsha McClemens, the chief's mom and the ex-wife of one of the richest men in the South, the late Joseph McClemens, Sr.

Capt. Valezquez: I thought the same thing, Lieutenant Dooley, but another thing that baffles me about Chief McClemens is why he would want a job as chief of police, which pays a little over a hundred thousand dollars a year. Besides, didn't his dad leave him and his mom some of those millions he made?

Mr. Dooley: I don't know, but now that we have contemplated this strange circumstance, I'm going to investigate and see if I can come up with some answers. As for now, I have to get across town to check on Jimmy, the little boy I was talking about earlier. You see, I promised his grandma that I would try to help get him back on track.

Capt. Valezquez: Alright then, Lieutenant; I gotta go, too . . . and if I hear of anything else in respect to what we just discussed, I'll get back with you.

Mr. Dooley: Thank you; that'll be great. Honestly, I could use an extra pair of eyes, ears, and hands, too. Goodbye, Captain Valezquez; I'll be in touch.

(They both exit the lounge and get into their vehicles. Mr. Dooley heads back over to M & M's Pool Hall to see if he can find anything on Jimmy's whereabouts . . . A few minutes later, he arrives at his destination. He exits his vehicle and enters the pool hall. Once inside, he is greeted by the youngman that he had spoken to in KFC's parking lot . . .)

Youngman: Hello, good to see you again, Officer Dooley.

Mr. Dooley: (recognizes the youngman's face) Well, hello to you too, young man. I never got your name because the last time we spoke, you ran off without further introducing yourself.

Youngman: Yeah, I know, and I'm sorry for running off like I did, sir, but I had to . . . (The guy suddenly stops, looks around, and whispers in Mr. Dooley's ear . . .) Can we go outside and talk?

Mr. Dooley: Yeah, sure; lead the way.

(Once outside, the guy commences to talk.)

Youngman: Excuse my peculiarity, Lieutenant Dooley, but I have to be very careful . . . especially when talking to a cop.

Mr. Dooley: It's okay, son, but before we converse, I'm going to have to ask you what your name is, just in case you decide to run off again.

Youngman: My name? . . . Uh . . . uh . . .

Mr. Dooley: What's the matter, son? You don't know your own name?

Youngman: Yes sir, I do

Mr. Dooley: Then why won't you tell me it? Is it because you have a warrant or something? Because if so, I'm not here to arrest you, okay?

Youngman: You're not? . . . Say you promise.

Mr. Dooley: What?! . . . Okay, young man, I promise not to arrest you.

Youngman: Alright, Lieutenant Dooley, I'll be straight with you. My name is Marvin Robinson, and I do have a warrant for my arrest.

Mr. Dooley: Okay then; now we're getting somewhere. Nice to finally meet you, Marvin . . . and what, may I ask, are you wanted for?

Marvin: Well sir, about six months ago, I was out riding with some friends, when a police officer got behind us and turned on his lights. My friend James, who was driving, had some unpaid traffic tickets and Michael, Earl and I had all been smoking pot. None of us wanted to go to jail, so everybody voted not to pull over. James sped off and a chase ensued from there. He kept going until there was enough distance between us and the officer. Then we all jumped out of the car and ran.

Mr. Dooley: So was anybody caught? Well obviously you got away.

Marvin: Well, Michael and I got away but Earl and James were caught. They went to jail that day, and they were already wanted for burglarizing some houses. Honestly, I didn't know anything about that because if I did, I wouldn't have gotten in the car with them. Anyway, Earl stayed in jail for ninety days. When he got out, he told Michael and I that James told the cops that I was driving the car that day. I wanted to turn myself in and straighten that lie, but I was afraid that I'd end up going to jail for a very long time, and I hate being locked up . . . So now what, Lieutenant Dooley? Are you still going to keep your promise?

Mr. Dooley: Of course I'm going to keep my promise. Not only that but, because you helped me with Little Jimmy, I'm going to have your file pulled first thing tomorrow morning and see who was the investigating officer on your case. Then I'm going to see if I can get that arrest warrant revoked.

Marvin: You would do that for me, Lieutenant Dooley? I mean, could you do that?

Mr. Dooley: I wouldn't tell you I could if I couldn't, son, and of course I'll do that for you. After all, from what I see and have come to know about you, Marvin, you really aren't a bad fella; but I do think you need to find some better friends to hang out with. Now on another subject, Marvin, I'd like to ask for your help one more time.

Marvin: Sure, Lieutenant; anything I can do to help you, just name it.

Mr. Dooley: Well, here's the deal, Marvin; last week, I took Little Jimmy back home to his grandma. Do you remember?

Marvin: Yes sir, I do; you're talking about June Bug.

Mr. Dooley: Yeah, that's him . . . Well, he's missing again, and his grandma doesn't seem to know where he is. You wouldn't happen to know anything or anybody who could help me find him, would you?

Marvin: Lieutenant, if anybody can get you that information, it's my friend, Earl. Ain't too much on the streets that he doesn't know or couldn't find out about, so if you want me to, I can take you to him and you can ask him if he knows where June Bug is.

Mr. Dooley: Yeah, if you don't mind, but is that safe? I mean, you won't get yourself in any trouble with this Earl guy, will you?

Marvin: Oh, nah! Earl's my boy; he and I have been friends since grade school. That's why he was mad at James for telling the cops that I was the one driving that car. Trust me, Lieutenant Dooley, if Earl can help me, he will.

Mr. Dooley: Okay, that's good enough for me. Can we go over there right now, then?

Marvin: Yeah, but can I ride with you? I'm riding my motor bike and I can't afford to get pulled over.

Mr. Dooley: Yeah, but do you want to leave your bike here?

Marvin: Yeah, it'll be okay. It's out back, behind the garbage can; I stash it there all the time.

Mr. Dooley: Okay, then hop in.

(Mr. Dooley and Marvin both get into the squad car and head down the street. Shortly thereafter, they arrive at Earl's house. Earl and Michael are hanging out in the driveway, shooting hoops. Mr. Dooley pulls up in the driveway. Fearing that he is there to arrest them, Earl and Michael both stop in their tracks with a look of desperation to run. As they turn and attempt to flee, Marvin exits the car and yells for them to come back, so they head back toward Marvin and Mr. Dooley . . .)

Marvin: (speaking to Earl and Michael while grinning) Hey there, fellas, what's going on?

Earl: Nothin', man, but you know what we say in the hood, "When you see the poe poe, don't be slow, 'cause you might end up going somewhere you don't wanna go." So we decided to skedaddle on out of here until we saw you.

Michael: Yeah, you know exactly how we do things around here, but what we don't do is bring the poe poe to our friends' homes, Marvin.

Mr. Dooley: Whoa, wait a second! Now first off, I am not here to arrest anyone, okay? . . . Anyway, who are you fellas and what are your names?

Michael: If I'm not under arrest, then why do you want to know my name, officer? I don't know who you are. In fact, I don't even know if you really are a police.

Mr. Dooley: That's true, young man, and I apologize for not properly introducing myself first . . . (Mr. Dooley takes out his badge and I.D. and shows them to Earl and Michael.)

Michael: Yeah, that's you alright, big head and all. (All three young men start laughing.)

Marvin: Oh yeah, Lieutenant Dooley, I forgot to tell you that Mike's the joker and prankster around here.

Mr. Dooley: Yeah, I can see that . . . Talking about me having a big head, I knew that was a joke.

Earl: I don't know Lieutenant Dooley, Michael might not have been joking because, now that he mentioned it, yo head is kinda big. (Everyone laughs again)

Mr. Dooley: Oh, so it's "Gang Up On A Police Officer Day", huh fellas? Well, I guess I'm going to be making an arrest afterall.

Earl and Michael: (speaking simultaneously) We were just playin' . . . our bad.

Mr. Dooley: (pretending to talk on his two-way radio) Officer needs assistance stat.

(Directs his attention to Earl and Michael.) Alright, I'm going to need both of you to get down on the ground and put your hands on top of your heads.

Michael: Man, you playin', right?

Earl: Dawg, you so stupid. You know . . .

Mr. Dooley: (interrupts Earl) Hey, does it look like I'm playing?! Now, I ain't gonna ask you all again; get down on your knees this instant, damn it!

(Both boys immediately drop to their knees and assume the position, as Marvin stands by and watches with a smirk on his face. Then Mr. Dooley turns to Marvin, grabs him, and commands him to get down as well. Now all three young men are on their knees with a look of fear and disbelief . . .)

Marvin: Sir, I thought you prom . . .

Mr. Dooley: (interrupts by yelling) Did I tell you to speak?!

Marvin: No sir.

Mr. Dooley: Then shut up! My backup will be here any minute now, and I don't want either of you to move a muscle. If you do, I'm going to have to shoot you.

(Seeing how fearful the young men appear, Mr. Dooley giggles. For he cannot restrain his laughter any longer. So, while yet laughing, he tells the boys that they can all get up . . .)

Marvin: Man, I told ya'll . . . I knew he was just playin'.

Michael: Yeah right, Marvin! Was that before or after you got down on your knees with those tears in your eyes?

(Mr. Dooley and Earl snickers.)

Marvin: Dawg, I was just going along with it to make it seem real for the Lieutenant.

Earl: Man, please! Yo butt was as scared as we were.

Marvin: Nah, I'm just sayin', though.

Michael: You just sayin' what, Marvin?

Marvin: Never mind, never mind . . . ya'll stupid.

(Everyone starts laughing at Marvin. Then Mr. Dooley begins speaking . . .)

Mr. Dooley: Alright, alright now fellas, let's all settle down here. I'm sorry for pulling one like that over on you guys but you left me no choice. Besides, I didn't know any other way to get ya'll to stop talking about my big head; that's a rather sensitive subject.

(All the boys laugh at that statement.)

Michael: It's okay, Officer Dooley, we ain't mad at you at all. As a matter of fact, I know Earl's not mad. He's just glad to know that going to jail is only a joke this time and not a reality.

(Everybody laughs.)

Earl: Now I know you ain't talking, "Mr. Get Arrested Every Quarter".

(Everyone laughs again.)

Mr. Dooley: Wow, I didn't know it was that serious, guys . . . I'm very sorry because if all that's true, then having to assume the position again must've been overwhelming . . . My bad, fellas. Will ya'll forgive me?

Marvin: Yes sir, it's all good.

Michael: Hold up, Lieutenant Dooley. Does this mean that you won't ever let that happen to us again?

Mr. Dooley: Nice try, son, but that's up to you guys . . . But you know what? I believe that you all can do it. If you need my help, I'll be glad to mentor you guys. Just remember your roles, okay?

(All three boys respond with a simultaneous "yes sir".)

Mr. Dooley: Now if you all don't mind, let's change the subject on a more sober note. As I've already told Marvin, there is a little boy missing. His name is Jimmy Nuttingham but he goes by the name of June Bug. Do you all know him?

Michael: Yeah, we know him.

Earl: Bug? Yeah, that's my boy. But how is he missing, Lieutenant Dooley? I just saw him last night.

Mr. Dooley: (*Glad to hear that Earl has* seen Jimmy, but curious about where he saw him) Did you say last night? Where'd you see Jimmy last night, Earl?

Earl: Well, I'll tell you Lieutenant Dooley, but you gotta promise me that, first of all, you won't tell anyone who told you this, and secondly, that I won't get any charges brought against me.

Mr. Dooley: Okay Earl, it's a deal, but I have two conditions as well. First, you and Michael must give me your real and full names. This is just for my own personal record, I don't like aliases.

And the second condition is that, henceforth, all three of you must work with me to help yourselves, Jimmy, and other young males get on the right track.

Earl: Hey, I ain't got no problem with that, Lieutenant Dooley. I'm tired of going to jail and I'm ready to get up out these streets anyhow.

Mr. Dooley: *(turns and looks at Michael and Marvin)* Okay, what about you two?

Michael: Can you throw in a little bonus with your offer, Lieutenant Dooley?

Mr. Dooley: That depends Michael . . . like what?

Michael: I got a little brother who's involved in what Earl is about to tell you. Will you promise me that you will let him be a part of this deal, and not send him off to jail?

Mr. Dooley: I don't know about that now Michael, because I don't know the whole situation. For all I know, Earl could tell me that someone has been murdered. I can't stop a person from going to jail on a murder charge, son. Even if it's self defense, that would be left up to a judge and a jury. But if it's not something that severe, then perhaps we could make some sort of arrangement for your brother. How about this, let's see what's going on and I'll give you a fair answer. Don't you guys trust me by now?

Michael: Yeah, we trust you and all, but not totally. Besides, even God tells us not to trust no man. I mean, I know it's okay to trust people like your parents, and I do trust my mom. I just don't trust my dad anymore because he ran off and left us. You know what I'm sayin', Lieutenant Dooley?

Mr. Dooley: Yes, I most certainly do, Michael and you are absolutely right. You see, if I could mentor a group of guys with those kinds of thoughts, I think we could make a very positive impact in the hood. So do we all have a deal here?

(Everyone nods in agreement.)

Earl: Okay, Lieutenant Dooley, I'm going to go ahead and fulfill my side of the bargain. My real name is Jeffrey . . . Jeffrey Pinkston, and Earl is my middle name.

Michael: And my name is Michael Autoro Sanchez. My little brother's name is John Allen Sanchez, Jr.; he's named after our no good father.

Mr. Dooley: *(Has a small notepad and is writing down their names as they speak)* Thanks for your cooperation, fellas, and I promise to do my best not to let you all down . . . trust me. Hopefully, you all will do the same for me. And for the record, Michael and Earl, Marvin has already given me his real name.

Michael and Earl: Yeah, we figured that when he pulled up in the car with you.

Mr. Dooley: Alright now Earl, let's hear what you know about Jimmy and Michael's little brother, John. And if you don't mind, I'll call you Jeffrey from now on.

Jeffrey: Yeah, that's cool. That way, if you do talk, maybe nobody will know that it was me who snitched.

Mr. Dooley: Now wait a minute son, don't go categorizing yourself as a snitch. Whenever you are doing something positive, you're doing the right thing . . . not snitching, okay?

Jeffrey: Yes sir, I gotcha. Alright, here's the deal. Last night, June Bug, Michael's little brother, and about five other little cats were down at M&M's Pool Hall, and Black took all of them in the back room with him.

Mr. Dooley: Who is Black, son? I told you I don't like aliases.

Jeffrey: Oh yeah, my bad! . . . Well, Jeremy . . . Jeremy Grayson, that's who took them in the back room.

Mr. Dooley: Okay, good. *(Mr. Dooley is still taking notes.)* Who is he? What does he do for a living?

Marvin: I can tell you, Lieutenant Dooley. Jeremy Grayson, AKA Black, is the manager of the pool hall. He's the one that was taking pictures of us when I met with you in the KFC parking lot. And from what I hear,he is Money Mike's right hand man.

Mr. Dooley: Alright, thanks for that information, Marvin; it's very helpful. Okay, you can finish the story now, Jeffrey.

Jeffrey: Okay. So he took Jimmy, John Jr., and the rest of them in the room with him, and when they came out, they all had backpacks.

Mr. Dooley: Alright. And do you know what was in the backpacks, Jeffrey?

Jeffrey: You mean you don't know, Lieutenant Dooley?

Mr. Dooley: Not really . . . I mean, I could assume that there were drugs inside but no, I don't know for sure. So why don't you just go ahead and fill me in on it, okay?

Jeffrey: Well, the word is, Money Mike don't like drug dealers so I doubt that you will find drugs in the backpacks, Lieutenant Dooley.

Mr. Dooley: So if it's not drugs, then what is it? Is it money? I mean, what else would they have kids carrying around in book bags?

Jeffrey: Duh! Books.

Mr. Dooley: Books?! What are you talking about? Are you telling me they're out there selling books?

Jeffrey: Not exactly, Lieutenant Dooley. You see, the books are props. Do you remember a movie called "Buck and the Preacher"? It was an old western movie about a preacher who always carried his Bible with him. Well, anyway one day these bad guys came up on the preacher while he was eating. They wanted to rob him, but the preacher asked them if he could at least keep his Bible, and the robbers honored his wish. So the preacher got his Bible, opened it up, and began to read a passage of scripture: "Though I walk through the valley of the shadow of death, I will fear no evil." Little did the robbers know, in the middle of the Bible, there were some pages cut out in the shape of a gun. That's where the preacher was hiding his piece. So he pulled out the gun and killed all of the robbers. The moral of the story is that you can't judge a book by its cover. Get it?

Mr. Dooley: Yeah Jeffrey, I get it the guy really wasn't much of a preacher. Anyhow son, now about this Black fella . . . Jeremy Grayson, is he the one that you said, that has these young boys out in the street selling guns?

Jeffrey: Yep, that's it. I see that it doesn't take you long to catch on, but it doesn't stop there, Lieutenant; it gets even more intriguing.

Mr. Dooley: Yeah? How so?

Jeffrey: After they sell the guns, they get to keep the money and do as they please with it.

Mr. Dooley: What?! Now hold on a minute, none of this is making any sense here. You mean to tell me that this guy, Jeremy, gives young boys book bags full of guns to sell, and that they get to keep the proceeds for themselves . . . No, I don't believe it; there's gotta be some sort of catch.

Michael: No, Lieutenant Dooley, Jeffrey's not lying. My little brother showed me what was in his back pack once, and then he gave Earl . . . I mean Jeffrey, and me some money.

Mr. Dooley: Wait a minute, let me get this straight, Michael. First of all, how old is John Jr.?

Michael: He's thirteen.

Mr. Dooley: Okay. And how much money are you talking about here?

Michael: Do you mean how much he gave us or how much he makes?

Mr. Dooley: Both, if you know.

Michael: Well, I'm not sure how much he makes but he gave me and Jeffrey two hundred dollars.

Mr. Dooley: What?! Your thirteen year old brother gave ya'll two hundred dollars?!

Michael: Yeah, two hundred each, so it was four hundred dollars all togethger.

Mr. Dooley: How old are you and Jeffrey?

Michael: Well, I'm nineteen and Jeffrey's twenty. He just had a birth day last week on June 23rd.

Mr. Dooley: What about you, Marvin? How old are you, and have you been getting a piece of the pie as well?

Marvin: I'm nineteen and no, unfortunately I didn't get any of the money. I make my money hustling at the pool hall. You see, I'm a pool shark, Lieutenant Dooley.

Mr. Dooley: Really? I'll just have to see about that later. Maybe we'll get a chance to see just how big a bite you have on the tables, Jaws.

Marvin: Cool, it's a bet; bring it on.

Mr. Dooley: Alright, back to this thing about selling guns. Tell me, Michael and Jeffrey, why would this guy have young kids like Jimmy and John Jr. selling guns for him? Why not you two?

Jeffrey: Well, for one, it would seem rather strange to see us, at our age. Walking up and down the street with back packs on, especially when there isn't a colledge near the area, wouldn't you say? And besides, we're smart enough to know that it's a federal offense. We ain't trying to mess with the F.E.D.S. It's bad enough dealing with you local cops.

Mr. Dooley: First off if you all are so smart, then you wouldn't let your little brother and friends go around selling guns or participate in criminal acts that you know to be a federal offense?

Michael: You think we didn't try doing that, Lieutenant Dooley? I love my little brother, it ain't nothing that I wouldn't do for him. And he loves me, too; that's why he shares his money with me and Jeffrey. But it's hard to convince these young dudes out here not to hang with Money Mike and his crew.

Jeffrey: Yeah, he's telling you the truth, Lieutenant Dooley. We've tried to tell him and Bug, but that guy Jeremy Grayson tells them that they don't have anything to worry about. Because they work for Money Mike, and he's untouchable. Everybody is starting to believe it, too, because every time Money Mike gets into it with the cops, he wins. He's never in jail for more than a couple of hours and whenever he has a confrontation with ya'll, he makes ya'll look stupid.

Mr. Dooley: Just how does he make us look stupid, son?

Jeffrey: Well, for instance, Michael and I were at the pool hall last week and we saw him throw you around like a rag doll. Even when the other cops came and started shooting, ya'll didn't catch him. Either ya'll can't shoot straight or he's just too good at dodging bullets. Anyhow, you know what I'm talking about, Lieutenant Dooley, you were there. He got away, didn't he?

Mr. Dooley: No, he hasn't gotten away, he just got by. I ain't going to lie, he threw me around like a lame duck, (all the boys laugh) but I promise you, his pay day is coming soon. I'm going to get Money Mike if it's the last thing I do. You see, he also frightened my son and brutalized his dog.

Marvin: I'd be careful about trying to get even with Money Mike if I were you, Lieutenant Dooley.

Mr. Dooley: (ignoring Marvin's statement) Alright, now where did ya'll say I could find Little Jimmy and John Jr.?

Michael: We didn't, sir.

Mr. Dooley: Okay, then if you know where they are, tell me.

Michael: Oh yeah, we know where they are Lieutenant Dooley, but I don't know if you wanna go over there by yourself. You see, Jimmy, John Jr. and the other five guys are all swimming over at Money Mike's crib.

Mr. Dooley: Right now?

Michael: Yes sir, right this minute.

Mr. Dooley: Are you sure, Michael?

Michael: 'Bout as sure as there is sugar in molasses.

(Jeffrey and Marvin laughs).

Mr. Dooley: Okay. So can you guys tell me the location?

Jeffrey: Not exactly.

Mr. Dooley: What do you mean, not exactly? Why not?

Jeffrey: Well, because we don't know exactly. You see Jimmy and John Jr. called us on the cell and told us where they were swimming, but we've never been there. If you want us to, we can follow them next time, though.

Mr. Dooley: Great idea, Jeffrey. Do you think that you all can do that without being detected?

Jeffrey: I don't know about that, but we can do it without them seeing us.

Michael: You see what I'm talking about Lieutenant Dooley, now that's why I support the United Negro College Fund, "Because a mind is, a terrible thing to waste".

(Marvin and Mr. Dooley laughs).

Jeffrey: What's so funny, ya'll?

Mr. Dooley: Is he serious?

Marvin: As serious as a heart attack.

Mr. Dooley: Alright guys, here's the deal: I don't want you all to mention any of this to anybody, especially Little Jimmy or John Jr.; we don't want them to tip off this Jeremy guy or Money Mike. And the minute you all see Little Jimmy and John Jr., give me a call ASAP, got it?

Jeffrey: Yeah, but don't you want us to call you as soon as we see them, Lieutenant?

Michael: Now, you see why they didn't want him, to sell the guns for them? Because of that type of stupidity . . . Sometime I wonder myself, why I'm still hanging out with him. (Marvin laughs).

Mr. Dooley: Okay now Marvin, I have to go. Do you need a way back to your bike?

Marvin: I'll be ah-ite, you go ahead and handle your business.

Mr. Dooley: Alright. Thanks for all of your help, guys. (He pulls out three business cards, which have his cell and office phone numbers on them. He gives them to each of the boys to contact him.) Now I'm out of here. Please keep me posted if anything comes up, okay?

(All three of them respond simultaneously, "Yes sir, we will." Then Mr. Dooley says goodbye. He gets into his car and drives off . . . About 20 minutes later, Mr. Dooley gets a call from his chief, Chief McClemens . . .)

Chief McClemens: Hello, Lieutenant Dooley, I'm calling to inform you that, as of right now, you are no longer authorized to perform police duties.

Mr. Dooley: Say what?! Chief, you must be bugging.

Chief McClemens: Yes, since you put it that way Lieutenant Dooley. As a matter of fact I am bugging. And let this little bug whisper something into your ear, there has been a warrant issued for your arrest.

Mr. Dooley: A warrant for my arrest?! May I ask why, sir?

Chief McClemens: For being insubordinate to your superior officer, and just for being a plain ole butt hole.

Mr. Dooley: Well, if that's the case, you should've been locked up years ago sir.

(Mr. Dooley hangs up the phone. He then dials his home to inform his wife of what Chief McClemens just told him, and to make sure that she and his kids are still protective custody. The phone is ringing and Mrs. Dooley is answering . . .)

Mrs. Dooley: (Knowing that it's her husband on the other end, Mrs. Dooley replies). Hello? Dooley's residence, may I help you? (Mrs. Dooley is being sarcastic because she is still upset about the prior argument she had with him earlier.)

Mr. Dooley: Hi honey, I know you're still mad and all but just hear me out, okay?

Mrs. Dooley: Yeah, you got that right, but go ahead, I'm listening.

Mr. Dooley: Anyhow, how are the kids? Is everything alright there? Are the officers still posted outside the house?

Mrs. Dooley: Enough with all the questions, Jonathan. I've known you long enough to know when something is wrong, so stop beating around the bush.

Mr. Dooley: Alright, sweetie. Um . . . how can I put this?

Mrs. Dooley: (yelling) To the point, Jonathan! Will you please just get to the point?!

Mr. Dooley: Okay I will, but please don't yell at me; not now, Lillian.

(Little Jay over hears Mrs. Dooley yelling at Mr. Dooley, so he interjects . . .)

Little Jay: Mama, why are you yelling at my dad like that? Diamerald told me that you guys had been arguing. I don't know why, but I do know that dad has a lot on his mind. He is trying very hard to find out who hurt Alofus, and now is definitely not the time for you to be mad at him, mom. So will you go easy on him, please? God has forgiven him for whatever he's done to upset you, so why can't you do the same?

(Mrs. Dooley is touched and astonished by Little Jay's sermon and immediately has a change of heart . . .)

Mrs. Dooley: Baby, you are absolutely right. I'm sorry for yelling at your dad. Now can we have a minute to finish our conversation?

Little Jay: Yeah ma, sure but if you need me, I'll be right over there (pointing).

Mrs. Dooley: Okay, son . . . Honey, are you still there?

(Talking to Mr. Dooley).

Mr. Dooley: Yeah sweetheart, I'm here. And just so you'll know, I'll always be here for you no matter what, because I love you.

Mrs. Dooley: (can sense something is wrong by Mr. Dooley's tone of voice) Honey, I want to apologize about this morning, I guess I let the devil get the best of me. Anyhow, I'm sorry and I love you, too . . . Now what were you trying to tell me?

Mr. Dooley: Chief McClemens has put out a warrant for my arrest.

Mrs. Dooley: Say what?! You gotta be kidding me! I know Chief McClemens hasn't done that to you . . . I mean, why would he? How could he?

Mr. Dooley: That's exactly how I felt when I heard it from the horse's mouth.

Mrs. Dooley: What charges does he have against you, sweetheart? Can he or does he have the authority to do that?

Mr. Dooley: Well, he and I haven't been seeing eye to eye lately, especially since I've been on that Satcher case. You know Dr. Satcher, the former professor at JSU. He died but it is rumored that he was murdered. Anyhow, Dr. Satcher and Chief McClemens were half brothers.

Mrs. Dooley: They were what? I thought Dr. Satcher was a black guy, and Chief McClemens is white.

Mr. Dooley: Duh! . . . Honey, you're acting like your sister, Kellie, now.

Mrs. Dooley: Alright now, I said I was sorry; don't make me angry again, Jonathan.

Mr. Dooley: Okay, you're right, I'm sorry. Anyway, to answer your question, he's charging me with insubordination to a superior officer . . . himself. And yes, of course, he does have the authority.

Mrs. Dooley: Well, who can over turn his authority, then? Because that's what we need done here, right?

Mr. Dooley: I'm not so sure, honey . . . Perhaps we can get some support from the city councilman or the Mayor.

Mrs. Dooley: Then, I'll just call Mrs. Adovis and ask her to get her husband to undo this mess.

(Mrs. Adovis is the Mayor's wife.)

Mr. Dooley: Aren't you forgetting something, honey?

Mrs. Dooley: What?

Mr. Dooley: Mrs. Adovis is Chief McClemen's mom, and she's married to Mayor Adovis.

Mrs. Dooley: Oh my God, you're right! It's been so long, and I'm not trying to involve myself with those people and their mess. So what are we going to do then, honey? We can't just sit back idly while they put you in jail and take your job away.

Mr. Dooley: No, we can't, but I have an idea. I'll give you Captain Valezquez's phone number. Maybe he could get us some help. Give him a call and let him know what's going on. He already knows about the dispute between the chief and I, so he will know what to do. But just in case I get locked up, don't tell the kids, okay honey? I wouldn't want them to get any more upset than they already are with the situation surrounding Alofus. And don't tell your sister Kellie either, for God's sake, or you might as well tell the whole world.

Mrs. Dooley: Okay, honey.

(They both hang up, and Mrs. Dooley calls Captain Valezquez. The phone is now ringing . . .)

Capt. Valezquez: (answering) Hello? Captain valezquez speaking.

Mrs. Dooley: How are you? This is Lillian Dooley, wife of Lieutenant Dooley. Do you remember him?

Capt. Valezquez: Dooley? . . . Dooley? Oh yeah, yes ma'am! I'm sorry, I was busy working on my wife's car, so I wasn't quite focused. Anyhow, what's going on, Mrs. Dooley?

Mrs. Dooley: Well, my husband asked me to contact you and inform you that his chief, Chief McClemens, issued a warrant for his arrest.

Capt. Valezquez: A warrant?! For the Lieutenant?! Chief McClemens must have lost his damn mind . . .

Oh, I'm sorry, ma'am. Excuse my language, but your husband is a good man, and it just makes me angry to hear that the chief would stoop that low to accomplish his own mission.

Mrs. Dooley: Oh, it's quite alright, I understand. I feel the same way, you just said it for the both of us. Anyway, what is this about his own mission, Captain Valezquez?

Capt. Valezquez: Never mind that statement, Mrs. Dooley, it will take too long to answer. So let's see here . . . is Lieutenant Dooley in jail now?

Mrs. Dooley: No, he's still free, but I don't know for how long.

Capt. Valezquez: Okay, then I'll give him a call myself. In the meanwhile, I don't want you to talk with Chief McClemens under any circumstances. Lieutenant Dooley told me that he had some protective officers posted outside your home. I'll call them to ensure that they don't let the chief persuade them to leave their posts.

Mrs. Dooley: Alright, I understand Captain Valezquez, and thanks, but please hurry. I'm worried about my husband's safety because, if you know him like I do, he can be rather stubborn when it comes to taking orders. I wouldn't want him to get into anymore trouble than he already has.

Capt. Valezquez: I can understand your concern, Mrs. Dooley but let's hope for the best, ma'am. And don't you worry, I'm going to do my best to right this wrong. As I said, your husband is a good man . . .

Oh, and one more thing, I need you to call an attorney who specializes in this sort of affair.

Mrs. Dooley: An attorney?! Do we really need an attorney right now?

Capt. Valezquez: Yes. We want to be sure that we are doing this thing by the book, so that they don't get away with anything.

Mrs. Dooley: Yeah, I guess you're right, Captain Valezquez; it would be in our best interest to get an attorney on board. My ex brother-in-law is an attorney, and he's pretty good, I might add. I'll have my sister, Kellie, to give him a call right away.

Capt. Valezquez: Good, but what type of law does he practice, Mrs. Dooley? Because we don't need just any ole attorney; we need someone who is criminally efficient and corporate savvy.

Mrs. Dooley: Then we're in luck. I think we have just what we need in my brother-in-law, Shawn Hogan. He is a political and corporate attorney who specializes in criminal corporate and political class action lawsuits.

Capt. Valezquez: Yeah, if you're right, it sounds like that's just the extra ammo we're going to need because we're dealing with some pretty powerful individuals here, Mrs. Dooley. Nevertheless, I need you to get on it right away. I'll get back with you as soon as I have something to move on.

(They both say goodbye and hang up . . . As Mrs. Dooley gets off of the phone, she turns and yells to her sister, Kellie, who is downstairs with the kids. For they are all still corralled for protection . . . Kellie is now responding to Mrs. Dooley's call. Mrs. Dooley heads downstairs to speak with Kellie face to face . . .)

Kellie: Lillian, did you call me, dear?

Mrs. Dooley: (now speaking to Kellie face to face) Yeah, I called you, Kellie. Could you come into the den with me? I need to discuss some important business with you and I don't want the kids to hear it.

Kellie: Sure, sis, but is everything okay? What's going on? You're spooking me.

(Mrs. Dooley and Kellie enters the den, closing the door behind.)

Mrs. Dooley: Okay, just calm down and lower your voice, Kellie. Like I said, I don't want to alarm the kids.

Kellie: Sorry Lillian, but please hurry and tell me what's going on. I'm a bit shaken up by the way you were calling out to me.

(Mrs. Dooley asks her sister, Kellie, to have a seat. Kellie sits down, and Mrs. Dooley begins speaking . . .)

Mrs. Dooley: Kellie, dear, I'm about to share something with you; it's not to leave this room. Is that understood?

Kellie: What is it, Lillian? Will you please just tell me? The suspense is killing me, and your procrastination is frightening me so much that I'm not certain whether or not I even want to know.

Mrs. Dooley: I understand because I'm scared too, sis. But I need you to promise me that nothing you and I discuss will leave this room, okay Kellie?

Kellie: Alright, you have my word, Lillian. Now for Pete's sake, what is it, sweetie?

Mrs. Dooley: Well, I don't know how to put this so I'm going to be straightforward. Jonathan has a warrant out for his arrest.

Kellie: (jumps to her feet in disarray) You're kidding me, right sis?

Mrs. Dooley: No Kellie, unfortunately not; it's true. Jonathan called me just a few minutes ago and informed me of the incident.

Kellie: Oh my God! What are we going to do, Lillian?

Mrs. Dooley: We're already on it, Kellie. Jonathan had me to call a friend of his on the force, a Captain Valezquez, and he is working on this situation as we speak. He also asked me to call an attorney. That's what I wanted to talk to you about. I know that you and Shawn haven't been collaborating much lately, but I need you to give him a call for us and tell him that we need his help.

Kellie: Lillian, now you know that Shawn and I haven't been on speaking terms ever since the child support and alimony hearing. He only communicates with Mark, but I can't help that; that is between him and God. I didn't do anything wrong to him; he was the one who did the cheating.

Mrs. Dooley: Kellie, right now I could care less about you all's on-going soap opera. We need Shawn's professional help, so please just get him on the phone, and I'll do the talking, okay?

Kelllie: Okay, I'll call him, but make sure you let him know that it was your idea and not mine.

Mrs. Dooley: Please, enough of the drama, Kellie. Just get him on the phone.

Kellie: Alright, don't get testy and make me lose my religion.

Mrs. Dooley: (smiling) Girl, if you don't hurry up and dial that number, that's not all you're going to lose. (They both laugh.)

(Kellie picks up the phone and dials her ex-husband, an attorney by the name of Shawn Hogan. Shawn practices corporate and political law, and is also a professor over at the local university (JSU) . . . The phone rings and a female answers on the other end. This is Shawn's secretary, Tiffany . . .)

Tiffany: Hello? JSU law pavilion, Professor Hogan's office, can I help you?

Kellie: Hi Tiffany, how are you? This is Kellie. Is Shawn in by any chance?

Tiffany: Oh, hi Ms. Hogan, I'm fine and you?

Kellie: I'm blessed, thank you.

Tiffany: Good. However, Professor Hogan is not in the office right now, but he should be returning shortly. Should I page him or leave a message?

(As she listens to the conversation, Mrs. Dooley nods to Kellie to have Shawn paged.)

Kellie: Yes Tiffany, dear. Would you please, if it's not too much trouble?

Tiffany: Why sure, Ms. Hogan, I'd be glad to. Is everything okay? Has Mark gotten into some sort of trouble?

Mrs. Dooley: (speaking quietly) No he's just fine, "Ms. Cravits".(Ms. Cravits being a nosy character from the hit television show "Bewitched").

Kellie: (snickers and motions for Mrs. Dooley to keep quiet) No, Mark is just fine. However, some other important issue has come up, so if you would, please have him call right away.

Tiffany: Yes, Ms. Hogan, right away ma'am.

Kellie: Thank you sweetie, and will you please inform him to contact me at my sister's home? And have a blessed day, okay Tiffany, dear? (They both say good-bye and hang up.)

Mrs. Dooley: Thank you Kellie, I really appreciate you doing this, but when he calls back, let me do the talking. I don't want you to piss him off before I can explain what's going on with Jonathan, okay?

Kellie: You mean if he calls back, don't you?

Mrs. Dooley: Oh he'll call back alright, because Tiffany, AKA "Ms. Cravits", is going to tell him that she believes that Mark is in some sort of trouble, but you refused to give her the info.

(Kellie and Mrs. Dooley both laugh at this statement. While they are laughing, the phone begins to ring. Kellie is apprehensive about answering the phone, so Mrs. Dooley motions for her to get it.)

Kellie: (picks up the receiver) Hello? Dooley's residence.

(The caller on the other end quickly responds. It's Kellie's ex-husband . . .)

Shawn: Hello? . . . Hello? . . . This is Shawn. Is that you, Lillian? . . . Where's Mark? Everything's okay, isn't it?

(Kellie is nervously and motionlessly holding the phone. Mrs. Dooley takes the phone and begins to speak . . .)

Mrs. Dooley: Hello Shawn; yes, this is Lillian. How's it going?

Shawn: Everything's just fine with me, Lillian, but what's going on there? Why is Kellie calling me from your house, and where is my son?

Mrs. Dooley: Whoa! Now hold on there, Professor. You're acting like you have me on the witness stand or something. Why don't you give me a chance to answer one question at a time?

Shawn: Well, where is my son?! Answer that one for me first.

Mrs. Dooley: Your son is here in my kitchen, stuffing his face, okay Shawn? And as for my sister, well she called you from my house because she's visiting, and I asked her to call you on my behalf.

Shawn: Okay Lillian, that's alright with me. And please forgive my rather erratic demeanor, but it was a bit awkward for my secretary to call and inform me to contact my ex at her sister's house, wouldn't you say?

Mrs. Dooley: Yeah, you're right Shawn, and I don't mean to be facetious but your third degree level of questioning was also rather abnormal, wouldn't you say?

Shawn: Alright Lillian, your point is well taken. Now about you having Kellie to call me, is there something I can help you with?

Mrs. Dooley: I thought you would never ask, Shawn, and now that you have . . . well, Mr. Intellectual, my favorite brother-in-law, I have a big favor to ask of you.

Shawn: Thanks for the compliments, Lillian, but I am your only brother-in-law and, in case you forgot, now I'm your ex brother-in-law.

Mrs. Dooley: No Shawn, I didn't forget but if you could, put away your selfish remarks for just a moment and take time to recollect something I told you prior to you all's divorce hearing.

Shawn: *(pauses briefly)* Oh yeah . . . are you referring to when you told me I would always be your brother-in-law, no matter what? Well, I thought you were just saying that to keep me from killing your sister. *(Shawn laughs, and Kellie over hears his remark . . .)*

Mrs. Dooley: No Shawn, I wasn't worried about that at all. I know how afraid you are of going to jail . . .

Kellie: (yelling in the background) Yeah, he is afraid to go to jail, and he used to fear going to hell too, but we know that all changed when he had that extra marital affair with you-know-who.

(The mood drastically transitions from comical to sober.)

Mrs. Dooley: *(while shushing Kellie)* Please, let me handle everything.

Kellie: *(yelling)* No! Don't you be shushing me, Lillian! What you need to do is tell your favorite brother-in-law to shut the hell . . . I mean, the heck up.

Mrs. Dooley: *(appalled by Kellie's language)* Kellie!

Kellie: Well, I'm sorry but ya'll are getting on my doggone nerves with all this reminiscing and playing the blame game.

Shawn: Lillian, if you don't mind dear, would you please put us on speaker mode? You may as well since we have all somehow gotten involved in a 3-way conversation.

Mrs. Dooley: Actually Shawn, I would mind; I don't think that would be a good idea.

Shawn: Why not? The litigation between the Hogans has begun, wouldn't you say?

Mrs. Dooley: Well, I guess you got a point, Shawn.

Kellie: What are you two talking about now, Lillian?

Mrs. Dooley: Shawn wants me to put him on speaker mode. Are you okay with that, Kellie?

Kellie: *(As Mrs. Dooley pushes the mode button to speaker phone)* Bring it on, sis, I think it's time I got the monkey off my back anyhow.

Mrs. Dooley: I believe he heard the monkey bit, Kellie.

Kellie: Why, good for him! He could always hear; the problem was getting him to listen.

Mrs. Dooley: Okay Kellie, on that note, I think I'm going to have to take a back seat for a minute and let you two handle this one.

Shawn: It's okay, sister-in-law, I'm not going to get into it with this argufier. She obviously hasn't gotten over her ardent love.

Kellie: Yeah right! I see you're still the carper and fancied dreamer that you always were.

Shawn: On the contrary, you were the argufying diva as I stated earlier, Kellie. You were just never able to tame this "monkey on your back", like you did the others, I suppose.

Kellie: What on earth are you talking about, Shawn? Just what are you implying here? You know that you were the only man in my life that ever meant anything to me, so where did all that come from?

Shawn: *(now stunned and mortified by Kellie's response)* You're right, Kellie and to be perfectly honest, I am being a complete butt-hole. I don't know why, because you certainly don't deserve any of this silliness coming from me. Will you please accept my deepest apology?

Mrs. Dooley: Girl, did you hear that? What are you waiting on? The man said he was sorry and wants you to accept his deep . . . est apology.

Kellie: I heard him alright, but does he mean it?

Shawn: Yes, Kellie dear, I mean it from the bottom of my heart.

Mrs. Dooley: Okay Kellie, I'm with you now girl. What's going on here, Shawn? Are you sick, or dying or something?

Kellie: No sis, the question is, has he died and been reincarnated? Because this is not the Shawn I know. He would never succumb like this, not in a million years.

(Shawn is now sniffling and actually appears to be crying.)

Mrs. Dooley: What's that noise, Shawn? Is someone else in your office, because I know that's not you I hear crying, is it?

Kellie: Girl please! That man has not cried a day . . . *(Kellie is interrupted with another sniffle)* . . . in his life.

Mrs. Dooley: Hold on a minute, Kellie, I believe he is crying. I'm sorry, Shawn; we didn't know. Was it something I said or was it my big mouthed sister? Please forgive us for our dense sense of humor. We are truly sorry but for God's sake, Shawn, please stop crying. I can't stand to hear a grown man cry.

Shawn: *(immediately stops crying)* Why not Lillian? Does the book of life forbid a man to cry?

Kellie: You mean the bible, don't you, Shawn?

Shawn: No, I mean the book of life, Kellie. You know, the one where God keeps records of all our works, whether they're good or bad.

Kellie: What do you know about God, Shawn?

Shawn: I know enough about him, Kellie: that he forgives and that he even gives us sinners another chance.

Mrs. Dooley: 'Sounds like Shawn went to the mountaintop and saw the burning bush, Kellie.

Kellie: Girl, the only bush that Shawn has seen burning, while being on top, is that thing between Carla's legs . . . And he tried to extinguish it with his little hose.

Mrs. Dooley: Kellie please, now that wasn't nice and I know God doesn't want you passing judgment on Shawn like that

Shawn: No, it's quite alright, sister-in-law. If they talked about Jesus, who had no sin, should I expect anything less of me, a sinner saved by grace?

Kellie: Did I hear you correctly? Saved? You, Shawn? If that's true, then I guess there will be peace in the valley after all. *(Mrs. Dooley laughs)*

Shawn: Yes Kellie, I have found the Lord . . . No, let me rephrase that. He was never lost but rather I, but now I am found, and after years of being blinded, I can see.

Mrs. Dooley: Wow, talk about a major attitudinal adjustment!

Shawn: No, Lillian my dear, it's a lot more than an attitude adjustment; it's also a heart renewing experience.

Kellie: I'd say! And now I'm convinced that God can, do the impossible. *(They all laugh at Kellie's remark.)*

Shawn: Very good joke, Kellie, except it doesn't matter if you're convinced or not because the third chapter of the book of Romans, verses three through through four clearly reads, "Let God be true and every man a liar".

Mrs. Dooley: Alright you guys, enough of the salvationist movement. Now can we just move along here in the flesh, and get back to what's happening here on earth?

Kellie: Yeah, you're absolutely right, sis. For a moment there, I thought we were experiencing the rapture or something.

Shawn: Okay, you two comedians, enough already. Now what was it that you wanted to discuss with me, Lillian?

Mrs. Dooley: After all the commotion here, I kind of lost my train of thought.

Kellie: *(being sarcastic again, yet sincere)* Why don't you start by telling him the truth, Lillian? That usually sets us free, if you know what I mean *(referring to the possibility of Jonathan getting locked up)*.

Mrs. Dooley: Yes, but of course Kellie, so I will begin with the truth. Shawn, Jonathan is in major trouble.

Shawn: Trouble?! Jonathan?! How so?

Mrs. Dooley: A warrant has been issued for his arrest.

Shawn: How has Jonathan, an arrestee, gotten himself positioned on the opposite side of the law? I'm sure this has to be a nail biting experience for you, Lillian.

Mrs. Dooley: Shawn, nail biting does not even come close to the adjective that describes this experience.

Kellie: Yeah, and the Neanderthal responsible for this catastrophe can stand to be called a few of those other adjectives right about now.

Shawn: Alright Kellie, let's not go there. Remember, vengeance belongs to God.

Kellie: I'm not talking about revenge or what I want to do to him, I'm only referring to his obvious character.

Mrs. Dooley: Okay Kellie, settle down, dear; let's keep focus here.

Shawn: If I may ask, who is this individual you both keep alluding to?

Mrs. Dooley: We're talking about your chief of police, Shawn.

Shawn: Chief McClemens?! Are you serious? I just met him at a fund raising banquet last week, and he seemed to be a very nice guy.

Mrs. Dooley: Well, after this type of action, it's quite evident that he's nefarious.

Kellie: I concur, as long as nefarious defines a dog or something.

Shawn: Not quite Kellie, but it does mean a wicked and villainous individual, if that suits you. And though I hear what you and Lillian are saying, we are not in a position to adjudicate such a matter; that's for the Almighty God to handle. However, if you are asking of my assistance, I will be more than happy to offer my services in the matter.

Mrs. Dooley: Why thanks for offering to help, Shawn but unfortunately, we are not in a financial position to reward your much needed services. To be honest here we are looking for your pro-bono services.

Shawn: Lillian, Jonathan needs my help, and you did say that I was your favorite brother-in-law. Helping a family member in the flesh is good, but to be able to help the family in the spirit, is an even greater reward than any monetary compensation could ever be. I'm ready to get started right away, so please accept my ex gratia services.

Kellie: For the record, Shawn, I'm so happy to see that you have truly experienced a transformation of the heart. And thanks for offering your support to my sister and her husband, Jonathan. God will bless you for this.

Shawn: He already has Kellie, he already has. Now I have a question for you, Lillian. Where is Jonathan right now? Has he been apprehended or turned himself in yet?

Mrs. Dooley: Neither. You know how hard headed Jonathan is, Shawn. The last thing he's going to do is turn himself in, especially when he feels that he is in the right.

Kellie: Yeah Shawn, why would Jonathan help them to incarcerate his self?

Shawn: Because it's the right thing to do, Kellie, even though you two might feel differently of the matter. By alluding the individuals seeking to apprehend him, he could possibly have more charges brought against him, thus limiting our chances of having this matter overturned. Even worse, he could get hurt or cause someone else's injury.

Mrs. Dooley: Well, since you put it that way, I'm inclined to agree with you. So what can we do to get this thing moving then, Shawn?

Shawn: First, have Jonathan to contact me ASAP, but not here at the office. Have him to call my cell, and I will take it from there. Meanwhile, you can just keep the prayers going. I gotta make a few calls to a couple of dignitaries who I feel we're going to need on board this band wagon.

Mrs. Dooley: Okay Shawn, I'll call Jonathan and have him to call you right away. Oh, I forgot to tell you that Jonathan had me to contact a Captain Valezquez. He will also be aiding us in this matter. Would you like to speak with him as well?

Shawn: Is he connected to Chief McClemens?

Mrs. Dooley: No, not directly. He's over the swat patrol unit, and he knows about the circumstances surrounding this ordeal.

Shawn: Good, that's what I needed to hear. So yes, please have Captain Valezquez to call me, Lillian.

Mrs. Dooley: Okay Shawn, I'll get on it right now. I hope to hear from you again shortly.

Shawn: No, better than that Lillian, I'm on my way over there to finish discussing this matter in person.

Mrs. Dooley: Great, we'll be happy to have you join us.

Kellie: *(talking to Lillian)* Did you forget something?

(referring to the protective officers posted outside the house)

Mrs. Dooley: Oh yes, I did forget. Thanks for the reminder, Kellie. *(Shawn is about to hang up, but Kellie's and Lillian's last statements entice him to remain on the phone . . .)*

Mrs. Dooley: Shawn, there is something else that I forgot to make mention of. We are all corralled here under police protection, per orders of Jonathan. I know you're wondering as to why, and rightly so. However Shawn, if you would please allow me to, I'll further explain this after your arrival. Meanwhile, I will let the officers know who you are and inform them of your visit, so you just come on over; I'm sure Kellie and Mark can't wait to see you.

Kellie: Alright sis, don't start no stuff.

Shawn: Okay Lillian, I'm on my way. And by the way, please don't tell Mark; I want to surprise him.

(Mrs. Dooley and Kellie both agree . . . And everyone says good-bye and hangs up.)

(Mrs. Dooley hangs up and heads to the front door to tell the officer that her brother-in-law, Shawn, is coming over to help deal with the situation surrounding Jonathan . . . Meanwhile, Mr. Dooley calls to inform Mrs. Dooley that he is being followed by fellow officers . . . Mrs. Dooley is now answering the phone.)

Mrs. Dooley: Hello honey, how are you?

Mr. Dooley: Well, not too good honey, because I have a couple of plain clothes on my tail.

Mrs. Dooley: Really?! Are you being pulled over?

Mr. Dooley: Not just yet sweetie, but I am about to go ahead and pull over in the Poe Pemp's parking lot, where I planned to meet with Captain Valezquez.

Mrs. Dooley: Did you say Captain Valezquez, honey?

Mr. Dooley: Yes, I did. Why?

Mrs. Dooley: Because if he's there, perhaps he can help you and keep them from arresting you.

Mr. Dooley: As a matter of fact, I think I see his squad car in the parking lot . . . Honey, do me a quick favor; dial his cell and let him know what's going on. Tell him that I'm outside in the parking lot right now.

Mrs. Dooley: Sure Jonathan, I'm calling him right now. (Mrs. Dooley hangs up on her husband and dials Captain Valezquez's cell phone . . . Captain Valezquez is now answering.)

Capt. Valezquez: Hello? Captain Valezquez speaking.

Mrs. Dooley: Hi there, Captain Valezquez. How are you? This is Mrs. Dooley. I'm gonna get right to the point; we don't have any time to spare. I know that you are there to meet with Jonathan. Well, he told me to let you know that he's outside in the parking lot right now, and he wants you to hurry out because he's being tailed by a couple of plain clothes men. I'm worried, so if you would, please have Jonathan to call me and let me know what's going on as soon as possible

Capt. Valezquez: Yeah, sure Mrs. Dooley, and I'm headed out the door as we speak. (Captain Valezquez is headed outside to meet with Lieutenant Dooley, and to see what's going on . . . As he dawns the door, he notices Lieut.Dooley getting out of his car. Simultaneously, a black Crown Vic with tinted windows pulls up behind the vehicle and two guys jump out and draw their weapons, commanding Lieut.Dooley to freeze, to keep his hands where they can see them, and to get down on his knees. (But Lieut. Dooley refuses to get down on his knees, however he does comply with the putting up his hands). Manwhile Captain Valezquez is walking out toward the arresting officers, hoping to attempt to rescue Lieut.Dooley.)

Capt. Valezquez: Hey! Hey wait! What's going on here, fellas?

(One of the officers turns and points his weapon towards Captain Valezquez and orders him to halt and put his hands up. Captain Valezquez does as the officer says. Then the other officer, paranoid of the situation, pushes his walkie-talkie's panic button and requests for back up. Within minutes, about eight other squad cars and unmarked cars pull up. Upon their arrival, several officers jump out and draw their weapons. Many of the officers recognize Lieut.Dooley and Captain Valezquez, which puts them in a state of disarray. We now have a precarious situation. For half of the officers on the scene are for Lieut.Dooley's apprehension and half are not.A sergeant from the swat team,by the name of Billy Johnson,speaks out to Captain Valezquez . . .)

Serg. Johnson: Hey Captain. What's going on here, sir?

Capt. Valezquez: Well, Sergeant Johnson, we have a rather sticky situation here. Those two officers (pointing) are here to arrest Lieutenant Dooley, but I'm not with it. I'll explain later. 'You with me?

Serg. Johnson: Yeah Captain, you know I'm your boy; I'm down for whatever.

(Now we have about twenty officers on the scene, some in plain clothes and some in uniforms. About twelve of them are in favor of Captain Valezquez and Lieut.Dooley . . . Things are appearing to get ugly, as everyone argues and aims weapons at each other. Suddenly, a voice shouts over a loud speaker, "Everyone be quiet and put away your weapons now; that's an order." It's the voice of Chief McClemens, who has just arrived on the scene . . .)

Chief McClemens: I'm only going to say this one more time, I want everybody to holster their weapons; that's an order.

(Everyone settles down and disgards their weapons. Chief McClemens walks over to Lieut.Dooley, who is now standing near Captain Valezquez . . .)

Capt. Valezquez: Chief McClemens, I'm glad you're here sir, but if I may ask, why is there an arrest warrant out for one of the finest officers on this force?

Chief McClemens: First of all, Captain Valezquez, we are all entitled to our own opinions. Secondly, I don't have to explain anything to you.

(Sergeant Johnson interjects . . .)

Serg. Johnson: Well, no disrespect sir, but my captain was just asking you to explain why one of our own was being treated like this. What, did he commit a murder or something? If not, which one of us hasn't done something amiss here?

Chief McClemens: Sergeant Johnson, you are way out of line; I am your superior and chief. One more outburst and I will deforce your badge.

Serg. Johnson: *(yelling)* Oh yeah?! Well, if this is the way this department is going to be run, you can have it!

(Lieut. Dooley attempts to calm the situation . . .)

Mr. Dooley: Alright hold on, everybody just hold on here a minute (looking at Captain Valezquez and then Serg Johnson). Thanks, Captain Valezquez and Sergeant Johnson, but this is my mess. I don't want you guys losing your badges over something I got myself into. Let it go, I'll be alright.

Capt. Valezquez: But Lieuteant Dooley . . .

Mr. Dooley: *(interrupting)* No, Captain Valezquez, I mean it; no more cunctation here. I'm ready to get this thing moving so that we can bring everything to the forefront.

Chief McClemens: Yeah, good choice, Lieutenant Dooley; it's about time you started making wiser decisions.

Mr. Dooley: Do you enjoy being a donkey, Chief McClemens?

Chief McClemens: If having you arrested labels me as that, then yes Lieutenant Dooley, I do enjoy being a donkey.

Mr. Dooley: I didn't really expect you to answer that, Chief McClemens. It was a rhetorical question, but of course you would answer it.

Chief McClemens: Whatever, Lieutenant Dooley. This is one refutation that will be rather cumbersome to explain your way out.

Capt. Valezquez: Don't worry, Lieutenant Dooley, I'll be a relater for you in this matter. As a matter of fact, I'm on it right now so keep your head up. We're gonna get this carrion resolved, just wait and see.

Chief McClemens: If I were you, Captain Valezquez, I wouldn't be so dire to jump on the band wagon with a self proclaimed renegade.

Capt. Valezquez: He's no renegade but he is a rather sedulous individual, and I believe that you motivated his degenerate action, Chief McClemens. You capriciously and arbitrarily lied on Lieutenant Dooley in order to issue his arrest warrant, but it's going to be very arduous for this case to be proven in a court of law.

Mr. Dooley: Thanks Captain Valezquez, but there's no need to discuss this matter with the chief because in due time, all that is necessary will be divulged to the entire city.

Chief McClemens: I am bombarded by you all's euphuistic discussion of me . . . but you know what? I could care less about the bombastic grandiosity coming from either of you; now take that to the bank . . . Oh, my bad, Lieutenant Dooley can't go to the bank because he's on his way to jail . . . Cuff him, Officer Jordan.

(Officer Jordan walks over to Mr. Dooley and asks him to turn around. Then he arrests him.)

Lieut Dooley: (turns to Captain Valezquez) Call my wife and let her know what's gone down.

Capt Valezquez: Okay, partner.

Mr. Dooley: Oh, and one more thing, Captain Valezquez: will you call Sergeant Willansby for me and bring her up to date on the matter?

(Sergeant Willansby and Captain Valezquez have been friends from years back in the academy.)

Capt. Valezquez: Sure thing Dooley, I'm on it right now *(dials Mrs. Dooley).*

Mrs. Dooley: Hello? Dooley's residence.

Capt. Valezquez: Hello, Mrs. Dooley; Captain Valezquez here.

Mrs. Dooley: Oh, hi there, Captain! What's going on with Jonathan? Is he okay?

Capt. Valezquez: Well, to be frank Mrs. Dooley, he's okay but he has been arrested and is on his way to jail right now.

Mrs. Dooley: Oh my God! No! Please tell me that you're kidding.

(Kellie listens in and over hears the bad news.)

Capt. Valezquez: No, Mrs. Dooley, unfortunately I'm not kidding. As a matter of fact, I watched them put the cuffs on him.

Mrs. Dooley: Wasn't there anything you could do to prevent them from taking him to jail?

Capt. Valezquez: Obviously not, since they got him, but it's not that I didn't try, Mrs. Dooley. It was a very indurate encounter, but in the end they prevailed.

Mrs. Dooley: What do you mean, prevailed? Who are you referring to, Captain Valezquez?

Capt. Valezquez: Our boss.

Mrs. Dooley: You all's boss? Are you talking about Chief McClemens or Major Stephens?

Capt. Valezquez: Oh, I'm sorry Mrs. Dooley; please forgive me for not being more specific, but I am referring to Chief McClemens. He's here on the scene right now.

Mrs. Dooley: Chief McClemens is there?!

(Kellie comments after over hearing the chief's name mentioned . . .)

Kellie: Sis, don't tell me that that scandalous, inebriated Chief McClemens is there.

Capt. Valezquez: Yes, I'm looking at him as we speak.

Mrs. Dooley: (gets emotional and begins to cry while speaking) You mean to tell me that this man hates Jonathan so much that he had to come down there and personally see him being apprehended?

(Kellie walks over to console her sister, Lillian . . .)

Capt. Valezquez: Please, Mrs. Dooley, don't stress yourself out over this situation. It's not the end of the world; trust me on this. We're going to get him out of this mess, okay?

Mrs. Dooley: Alright Captain Valezquez, thanks, but are you sure this thing can't get any worse?

Capt. Valezquez: Well, I should think not, unless of course, there is some unforeseen occurance.

Mrs. Dooley: Good, I certainly hope there's not one of those. And oh yeah . . . Captain Valezquez, I almost forgot; I did get in touch with my brother-in-law, the attorney.

Capt. Valezquez: Great. Did you bring him up to par as to what's going on?

Mrs. Dooley: Yes, as much as I could. However, I didn't inform him of Jonathan's incarceration because, as you know, he wasn't locked up at the time.

Capt. Valezquez: That's okay. So what did he say after you informed him, and will he be charging you all for his services?

Mrs. Dooley: He feels the same as we all do about the matter and no, he's not charging us for his services. He's on his way over right now to discuss the specifics in more detail. He and Jonathan are pretty close.

Capt. Valezquez: Okay, that's good news, Mrs. Dooley. Now here's what I would like for you to do for me: Have your brother-in-law to give me a call as soon as he gets there. Meanwhile, I'll head downtown to the station to see what's going on with Lieutenant Dooley.

Mrs. Dooley: Alright, I will have Shawn to call you the minute he gets here. And yes, please hurry and check on my Jonathan.

Capt. Valezquez: Sure thing, Mrs. Dooley, and I'll have him to call you ASAP. 'Talk to you guys soon, I hope.

Mrs. Dooley: Yes, and so do I.

(Soon after Mrs. Dooley hangs up, Kellie inquires of her as to what happened with Jonathan.)

Mrs. Dooley: Well sis, Jonathan was headed to the Poe Pemp's restaurant to meet with Captain Valezquez, and he was being followed by a couple of officers. When he got out to go inside the restaurant, they arrested him. Captain Valezquez tried to rescue him from the situation but, as you know, Chief McClemens showed up and ordered the arrest to continue. (Mrs. Dooley is starting to get a bit upset again.)

Kellie: Everything's going to be alright sis, don't worry. Shawn is en route, and it shouldn't be long before Jonathan's back home, okay dear?

Mrs. Dooley: Oh, I know Kellie, I'm just overwhelmed right now, especially with all that has gone on with Little Jay, Mark and Alofus . . . not to mention the situation that Sergeant Willansby was in.

Kellie: Yeah sis, I understand. And even though you're weeping now, it will only be for a night. Remember, joy comes in the morning, sweetheart.

Mrs. Dooley: Ah, that was kind of you to recite such poetic words, Kellie, and very well put I might add.

Kellie: Anytime Lillian, you know you're my girl. Now let's go into the kitchen and get a bite to eat before we both dwindle away. (They both laugh and mosey on off to the kitchen, where the kids are.)

(Meanwhile, as Captain Valezquez drives over to the city jail, he decides that this would be a good time to call Sergeant Willansby, in regards to Mr. Dooley's request, so he dials her number. The phone rings and Sergeant Willansby answers . . .)

Serg. Willansby: Hello? Sergeant Willansby here.

(Sergeant Willansby is still in the hospital (St. Mary's), but ironically she is scheduled to go home today.)

Capt. Valezquez: Yes, and hello to you too, Sergeant Willansby. How are you doing, young lady? It's been a long time since we last spoke.

Serg. Willansby: (not really sure who she is speaking with) I am doing much better; thank you for asking. And I suppose that it has been a while because, to be honest, I don't even know who this is, so if you would be so kind, indulge me with your name.

Capt. Valezquez: Oh, my bad . . . This is Dennis, Dennis Valezquez, JPD swat commander.

Serg. Willansby: Dennis? Is this Dennis "Doughboy" Valezquez? Oh my God, what a surprise to hear from you! But how on earth did you get my number?

Capt. Valezquez: No, you didn't call me out like that! Doughboy? Okay it's cool, but since we're going there, what's up "Sweet Pea" Willansby?

Serg. Willansby: (starts laughing and Captain Valezquez joins in) Yeah, you're Doughboy alright. So Dennis, how has it been, and what's going on with you now?

Capt. Valezquez: Well if you gotta know, honestly, things were indubitably quiet before we were dispatched to rescue you from those nefarious hoodlums.

Serg. Willansby: Silly boy, I was referring to your personal life, but you always were an industrious kind of person. Anyhow, thanks for the rescue but again, how did you get my number, Dennis?

Capt. Valezquez: Okay, that's another story. I was acquainted with a friend of yours during the rescue, a Lieutenant Dooley. Well, he was the one who called me in on the mission, you see?

Serg. Willansby: Yeah, Jonathan? He's a friend of mine and then some, but I won't get into that. Why would he give you my number, though?

Capt. Valezquez: Well Sergeant Willansby, on a more sober note, Lieutenant Dooley has gotten himself into some trouble.

Serg. Willansby: Trouble?! What type of trouble, Dennis?

Capt. Valezquez: You mean you haven't heard?

Serg. Willansby: *(now a bit emotional and anxious to hear what's going on)* Dennis, will you please just get to the point? Enough with the pity-pat questions, okay?

Capt. Valezquez: Alright, then he's been arrested.

Serg. Willansby: Been arrested?! Who are you talking about, Dennis? Because I know that you can't be referring to Jonathan.

Capt. Valezquez: Unfortunately, I am Sergeant Willansby, and he wanted me to call and inform you.

Serg. Willansby: Well I mean, how could this happen to such an outstanding and model lieutenant?

Capt. Valezquez: That's exactly how I feel about the matter. However, Chief McClemens obviously thinks otherwise; he even called Lieutenant Dooley a renegade.

Serg. Willansaby: A renegade?! Chief McClemens?! What does Chief McClemens have to do with this?

Capt. Valezquez: Everything; he has everything to do with this, Sergeant Willansby. He's the one who orchestrated the whole thing. As a matter of fact, I personally witnessed Lieutenant Dooley's apprehension, and Chief McClemens ordered the arrest.

Serg. Willansby: On what grounds was the arrest warrant issued?

Capt. Valezquez: Insubordination and something about disrespecting his superior, I believe. Actually, I'm not certain; that's why I'm on my way downtown now.

Serg. Willansby: Since when is it against the law to disobey your superior?

Capt. Valezquez: I don't know, it sounds fakey to me too, Sergeant Willansby. Nevertheless, they have gotten away with it, at least for now. Anyhow, I'll call you back, okay?

Serg. Willansby: Alright, please do and keep me posted. Meanwhile, I have a few calls to make. 'Talk to you soon. (They both hang up.)

(Captain Valezquez pulls up at the police station and heads inside to check on Mr. Dooley's status and arrest. After entering the station, he walks toward the counter and is greeted by Major Valerie Stephens, a middle-aged, black female who is in charge of jail operations at the police station . . .)

Maj. Stephens: *(while smiling)* Hey there, Capt Valezquez, what's going on with you and the other gun bunnies these days?

Capt. Valezquez: Well, hello to you too, Major Stephens. Actually, things were moving along just fine until the uncanny event that recently went down.

Maj. Stephens: And what, may I ask, went down Captain Valezquez?

Capt. Valezquez: You mean you haven't heard yet?

Maj. Stephens: Heard what?

Capt. Valezquez: Your boss had Lieutenant Dooley arrested.

Maj. Stephens: Lieutenant Dooley?! You're kidding me, right?

Capt. Valezquez: I wish I was kidding, Major Stephens, but unfortunately I'm not; it's true. I witnessed it myself about an hour or so ago. *(Now Captain Valezquez has a look of perplexity on his face, wondering why the major wasn't informed about Mr. Dooley's arrest since she is supervisor over the jail.)* Haven't they brought him in?

(With an honest look of surprise, Major Stephens puts her finger to her lips, as to signal Captain Valezquez to hush. Then she tells him to follow her into her office. Befuddled, Captain Valezquez does as he is told. Major Stephens is now speaking to him in private . . .)

Maj. Stephens: Let's get one thing straight here, Captain Valezquez, Lieutenant Dooley and I are friends, okay? And the last thing I would want is for him to get arrested. Honestly, until now, I hadn't even known that there was a warrant for his arrest. So tell me, Captain Valezquez, what's really going on here?

Capt. Valezquez: Well Major Stephens, to be perfectly honest, I'm not completely sure but I believe that Chief McClemens and a guy by the name of Dr. Elenski are involved in CCE. The FBI is gathering substantial evidence against them as we speak, which I hope will prove subserve in the ongoing investigation.

Maj. Stephens: Excuse my ignorance, Captain Valezquez, but what exactly does all this have to do with Lieutenant Dooley's arrest?

Capt. Valezquez: Indirectly, it has a lot to do with it. You see, ever since Lieutenant Dooley and Sergeant Willansby started their investigation on the Satcher case, they have both been deemed as Chief McClemens' foes, which is why Sergeant Willansby was kidnapped and Lieutenant Dooley has now been arrested. And anyone who decides to aid them in the investigation could also be possible targets, so I guess I'm on that list by now.

Maj. Stephens: Well, you can count me in too then, Captain Valezquez, because there's no way that I'm going to sit back and watch this falsity surrounding my dear friend evolve. Now which officer cuffed Dooley, Captain Valezquez? You said that you witnessed it, and I would like to know who it was so that I can radio him and see why Lieutenant Dooley hasn't been brought in yet.

Capt. Valezquez: I believe it was Officer Jordan.

Maj. Stephens: Are you talking about Melvin Jordan? Doesn't he work in the homicide division?

Capt Valezquez: Yeah. I didn't pay that any attention but now that you mention it, it was rather strange for a homicide cop to have been on the scene. As a matter of fact, Officer Davenport was there too and she also works in homicide. I believe that both she and Officer Jordan were the ones following Lieutenant Dooley when he met me at the Poe Pemp's restaurant. Now I'm getting even more worried, Major Stephens, so hurry and call Officer Jordan so we can see what's going on with the transport.

(They both walk out of the office. Major Stephens walks over to the switchboard and asks the attending officer to get Officer Jordan on the radio. The officer tries but to no avail. For some unapparent reason, Officer Jordan is not responding to the call. This is very odd and eerie, especially considering that the excursion was from Poe Pemp's {where the arrest took place} to the police station. Captain Valezquez and Major Stephens are both frantic at this point . . . Suddenly, a 1024 comes in over the radio, stating that an officer is down and needs assistance stat, so Captain Valezquez and Major Stephens head out to aid the officer . . .)

(They have arrived at the designated location and are approaching several uniformed officers and a couple of undercover detectives, who are all standing around, looking downward. An ambulance is now pulling up at the scene. Two E.M.T.'s jump out, grab the gurney, and rush over to where everyone is corralled.

Major Stephens and Captain Valezquez hurry over to the scene to inspect . . . To their surprise, they find Officer Jordan lying there in a pool of blood. He is unconscious. As the E.M.T.'s frenetically work on him, Major Stephens and Captain Valezquez walk up to one of the officers, Officer Jacelyn Davenport. Officer Davenport is a black female, who is sitting in the unmarked police car that Officer Jordan transported

Mr. Dooley in. Officer Davenport is holding her head down, looking sorrowful as Major Stephens questions her . . .)

Maj. Stephens: Hello, Corporal Davenport, are you okay? What happened here?

Corp. Davenport: Yes, Major Stephens ma'am, fortunately I am okay, but my partner, Officer Jordan, wasn't so lucky.

Maj. Stephens: What do you mean? What exactly went down here, Corporal?

Corp. Davenport: Well ma'am, Officer Jordan and I were en route downtown, transporting Lieutenant Dooley to the station, as Chief McClemens ordered. And as we turned on to Obama Boulevard, a big truck abruptly stopped in front of us, causing Officer Jordan to rear end it. We dismounted our vehicle and then, a black SUV pulled up beside us. About three or four armed guys jumped out, ordering us to surrender our weapons. Officer Jordan then drew his revolver and started shooting at the perps. I joined in but we were out numbered. I believe Officer Jordan struck one of the individuals but it didn't seem to hurt him because he walked right up to Officer Jordan, grabbed him, took his revolver and shot him in the head with it. By then, I was in shock. I turned to shoot the guy but he just looked at me and told me to put my gun away before someone else got hurt. Of course I was baffled at his statement, but I proceeded to open fire and he just laughed. Then he threw Officer Jordan about 20 feet to where he now lies. I turned and ran inside that building (pointing), afraid that I was being pursued. Then I hid and called for backup. When all the other officers arrived, I came out to find Officer Jordan lying in blood, and Lieutenant Dooley was nowhere to be found, ma'am *(starts to cry)*.

Capt. Valezquez: *(now enraged, grabs Officer Davenport)* What?! Lieutenant Dooley is missing? How can that be?! You were all supposed to transport him to jail, and now he's gone?

Maj. Stephens: *(pulling him away from Officer Davenport)* Hold on here, Captain Valezquez. Please settle down and get a hold of yourself. Let's handle this properly.

(Captain Valezquez walks back over to the E.M.T.'s, who have loaded Officer Jordan into the ambulance and are now pumping on him hysterically, trying to recessitate him. As he turns and heads back to Major Stephens, he is approached by Eddie Lansing, the officer who found Alofus after he had been injured . . .)

Offc. Lansing: Hey there, Captain Valezquez, how are you? May I have a word with you, sir?

Capt. Valezquez: Yes, Officer Lansing, what is it?

Offc. Lansing: No, not here sir, in private please.

Capt. Valezquez: Alright then, but where?

Offc. Lansing: In there (pointing at the building that Officer Davenport ran into during the assault).

(They both enter the building and begin to talk . . .)

Offc. Lansing: Well sir, I hope that I'm doing the right thing, discussing this with you because right now, I don't know who to trust around here.

Capt. Valezquez: What are you talking about, Officer Lansing?

Offc. Lansing: I'm talking about staying alive, sir. It seems like everybody who works against that guy either winds up hurt or dead.

Capt. Valezquez: And what guy is that, may I ask?

Offc. Lansing: The same guy who threw Lieutenant Dooley around in the pool hall. You know, the one who everybody's afraid of. I believe he calls himself Money Mike.

Capt. Valezquez: Money Mike?! What about him, Officer Lansing?

Offc. Lansing: He was the one who ambushed Officer Jordan and Officer Davenport, him and his comrades, sir.

Capt. Valezquez: And how do you know that, Officer Lansing?

Offc. Lansing: Because I was the first one on the scene, and when I walked over to Officer Jordan, he was still responsive. I asked him who did that to him and he told me that it was the same guy who jumped out the window at the pool hall.

Capt. Valezquez: Are you sure about this?

Offc. Lansing: Yes sir, I'm sure I heard Officer Jordan say it was Money Mike, but whether or not he was sue, I can't answer.

Capt. Valezquez: Okay good. Thanks, Officer Lansing, this is very helpful information and I need to get it to Major Stephens right away.

Offc. Lansing: Major Stephens, sir? Can you trust her?

Capt. Valezquez: Yes, she can be trusted. And I don't mean to be rude but right now, I'm in a hurry. I'll be in touch. Don't disclose this info to anybody else. Is that clear, Officer Lansing?

Offc. Lansing: Very clear sir; you don't have to tell me twice. Good luck.

(Captain Valezquez and Officer Lansing both exit the building and go their separate ways . . .)

(Captain Valezquez has walked back to Major Stephens, who is now speaking to him.)

Maj. Stephens: So there you are. Where did you run off to?

Capt. Valezquez: Oh, I'm sorry ma'am, were you looking for me? I walked over to see how Officer Jordan was doing and then, I was approached by Officer Lansing, who provided me with some very pertinent information.

Maj. Stephens: As a matter of fact, Captain, I was looking for you. Now what info did Officer Lansing give you that was so pertinent?

Capt. Valezquez: Well, he was able to get Officer Jordan to tell him who assaulted him before he blanked out.

Maj. Stephens: Really?! That's good news! And who did he say assaulted him?

Capt. Valezquez: He said it was the same guy that I encountered at the pool hall, not too long ago.

Maj. Stephens: How was he able to determine that, Captain Valezquez?

Capt. Valezquez: Because when I called for backup, he was one of the responding officers, and he got a good look at the guy.

Maj. Stephens: Okay great, then what are we waiting on? Let's put an APB out on the perp and go get him.

Capt. Valezquez: An APB, ma'am?! He's been on our most wanted list and the FBI's for quite some time now, and from my understanding, he isn't exactly the kind of individual who will come along quietly.

Maj. Stephens: Really? Who is he, Captain?

Capt Valezquez: He's the legendarily savage perp, Money Mike. He has been causing quite a bit of chaos for most law enforcement throughout the country, and my understanding is that he, Chief McClemens, and Dr. Elenski are all in cahoots.

Maj. Stephens: Money Mike?! Captain, if he is truly the one who abducted Lieutenant Dooley, then we've got more of a problem than you care to know. And if Chief McClemens is in partnership with that criminal, then we have an even bigger problem. But who is Dr. Elenski?

Capt. Valezquez: Dr. Elenski is a former professor of JSU. He was fired by the then president of JSU, a Dr. David Satcher, who ironically passed away soon after Dr. Elenski's termination. Some individuals believe that Dr. Elenski had some involvement with his death, despite the fact that he was never a suspect. But never mind that, Major Stephens; what is all this hoopla surrounding Money Mike? I've been hearing bits and pieces about him being untouchable.

Maj. Stephens: First of all, I wouldn't exactly call the clamor surrounding Money Mike "hoopla", but in relation to him being untouchable, that's true so far. I mean, you just said it yourself: Not only is he vexing law enforcement throughout the country, he even has the FBI looking for him, so he's reasonably untouchable. Wouldn't you say, Captain?

Capt. Valezquez: Well, since you put it that way Major Stephens, I guess so. Anyhow, enough gossip about that vivacious entity. I need to locate Lieutenant Dooley before something happens to him; I promised Mrs. Dooley that I would look out for him.

Maj. Stephens: I concur, Captain, good luck. Meanwhile, I'm headed back to headquarters to see what I can do from that end. Keep in touch, okay?

Capt. Valezquez: Roger that, ma'am.

(Major Stephens and Captain Valezquez depart in their squad cars. While driving, Captain Valezquez searches for the vehicle in which Money Mike and his partners may be carrying Mr. Dooley. Captain Valezquez decides to give Mrs. Dooley a call, to inform her of what's going on . . .)

Mrs. Dooley: Hello? Dooley's residence.

Capt. Valezquez: Hi, Mrs. Dooley; Captain Valezquez here again, ma'am.

Mrs. Dooley: Oh, hi there, Captain Valezquez. Is there any good news? Because right now, I can't bear to hear any more discouraging news.

(After hearing Mrs. Dooley's rather adamant statement, Captain Valezquez is reluctant about expelling the bad news regarding Mr. Dooley's abduction. Nevertheless, he knows that it is the right thing to do.)

Capt. Valezquez: Well, Mrs. Dooley, I hate to be the bearer of bad news . . .

Mrs. Dooley: *(immediately interjects)* No, don't tell me, I don't want to hear it.

(Thinking that Captain Valezquez is about to tell her something horrid about her husband, Mrs. Dooley dolefully drops the phone, walks over to the recliner, sits down and starts to cry with her hands concealing her face.

Kellie immediately rushes to her aid. She picks up the phone with one hand and places the other on Mrs. Dooley's shoulder . . .)

Kellie: *(on the phone, while consoling Mrs. Dooley)* Hello? Hello? Are you still there, Captain Valezquez?

Capt. Valezquez: Yes, I'm still here. Who am I speaking to, and what's going on with Mrs. Dooley?

Kellie: This is Kellie sir, Mrs. Dooley's sister. What on earth did you say to her?

Capt Valezquez: Hi Kellie. To be honest, I didn't get to tell her much of anything, except that I hate to be the bearer of bad news. It was then that she yelled for me not to tell her and, I guess, threw the phone down.

Kellie: Well, if she's carrying on like this when you haven't even disclosed the bad news, I'm not sure if we should tell her just yet, but I suppose we're going to have to eventually. By the way, what is the bad news, Captain Valezquez?

Capt. Valezquez: Are you sure you want me to tell you, Kellie? I mean, do you think it's okay to discuss this while she's already upset?

Kellie: Yeah, I'm sure. We need to know what's going on here . . . Okay Captain Valezquez, I'm walking into the other room now. You can go ahead and tell me; I'll break the bad news to my sister.

Capt. Valezquez: Alright then Kellie, if you say so, but if things should get out of hand, remember that it was your idea, okay?

Kellie: *(yelling)* Okay, I take full responsibility; just tell me already!

Capt. Valezquez: Alright, alright, just settle down . . . Lieutenant Dooley is missing and we don't know where he is right now.

Kellie: *(yelling)* What?! Missing?! How on God's green earth is Jonathan missing? Just about an hour or so ago, you called to tell us that he had been arrested, and that he was on his way to jail.

Capt. Valezquez: Kellie, please lower your voice. We don't wanna alarm your sister; she's already upset.

(After hearing Kellie yell, Mrs. Dooley walks into the room that Kellie's in. Kellie looks at the doorway and sees her.)

Kellie: Too late Captain, she's right here, looking me in the eye and reaching for the phone.

Capt. Valezquez: *(nervous about having to tell Mrs. Dooley this info)* No Kellie, don't give her the ph . . .

(He is interrupted by Mrs. Dooley.)

Mrs. Dooley: Why not, Captain Valezquez? What are you afraid to tell me?

Capt. Valezquez: It's not that I'm afraid to tell you, Mrs. Dooley. I'm just concerned about your health, and how you will react to . . . (interrupted by Ms. Dooley again)

Mrs. Dooley: To what? Hearing that my husband is missing? Yeah, I over heard my big mouthed sister yell it out. All I want to know is whether or not he is alright and if you all will get him back, Captain.

Capt. Valezquez: Well, to be honest ma'am, I can answer one question with assurance. And that is, we will get him back. As to whether or not he's okay, we don't know at this point.

Mrs. Dooley: Alright Captain Valezquez, I understand; fair enough. Just call me back when you all find my Jonathan. Until then, I'm not interested in talking to JPD. Is that understood?

Capt. Valezquez: Yes ma'am, I understand and I can assure you that we will do everything in our power to apprehend the culprits responsible for this outrageous catastrophe.

Mrs. Dooley: Of course you will. I wouldn't expect anything less, seeing how diligent you all have been working so far (being sarcastic).

Kellie: (Over hears Mrs. Dooley's sarcastic remark) Now Lillian, that's not nice. Captain Valezquez has been nothing but a friend, and has been working overtime to help resolve this mess.

Mrs. Dooley: Yeah, you are absolutely right, Kellie. Captain Valezquez, I want to apologize. I guess I let my emotions get the best of me. Please accept my deepest apology.

Capt. Valezquez: There's no apology necessary, Mrs. Dooley; no harm was done. I understand perfectly. I probably would have reacted the same way if Mrs. Valezquez was missing, so don't beat yourself up, okay?

Mrs. Dooley: Why thanks for your consideration and understanding heart, Captain Valezquez.

(Their conversation is interrupted by one of the protective officers who were posted outside, Officer Douglas . . .)

Offc. Douglas: Hi Mrs. Dooley. Sorry to interrupt, ma'am, but you have a visitor. I believe it's the young man that you were expecting.

Mrs. Dooley: *(talking to Captain Valezquez)* Please excuse me for a moment.

(Holding her phone down from her ear, she responds to the officer) Officer Douglas, did he say that his name was Shawn Hogan?

Offc. Douglas: Yes ma'am, that's who he introduced himself as.

Mrs. Dooley: Oh great! That's my brother-in-law, the attorney. Pl
see him in right away. (She returns her attention to Capta
Valezquez and puts the phone back to her ear) Okay, Captai
Valezquez, I'm back. Please forgive the interruption, but Officer
Douglas was letting me know that my brother-in-law, Shawn,
has arrived.

Capt. Valezquez: Good news. I'd like to speak with him as soon as he
gets inside, if that's okay with you, Mrs. Dooley.

Mrs. Dooley: Sure. As a matter of fact, he's walking through the door
right now. I'll give him the phone.

*(Shawn joins Mrs. Dooley and Kellie in the room. Mrs. Dooley greets him
with a hug as Kellie looks on, debating whether or not she should do the
same. She hesitates as Shawn walks up to hug her but surprisingly, she hugs
him back.)*

Shawn: Don't worry, Kellie, I won't bite and you don't have to worry
about catching any diseases.

(smiles while saying this)

Kellie: Oh, I'm not the least bit worried about the bite Shawn, but I
am a little skeptical about the diseases. *(She and Mrs. Dooley
both laugh.)*

Shawn: *(sarcastically replies)* Alright you two, very funny; ha, ha.

Mrs. Dooley: Oh Shawn, I almost forgot; the captain that I told you
about—you know, the one that's working to help us with
Jonathan—is on the phone. He wants to speak with you right
away.

(Mrs. Dooley hands the phone to Shawn.)

: Hello? Shawn Hogan here.

t. Valezquez: Hi, Mr. Hogan, how are you doing sir? I'm Captain Valezquez, a friend of the Dooleys. My understanding is that you are an attorney.

Shawn: Yes, Captain, that's correct.

Capt. Valezquez: Good, because we're going to need some good legal advice in the matter at hand. Has Mrs. Dooley informed you of what's going on?

Shawn: Yes, I believe so, but to a certain extent. I'm indeterminate as to whether or not she conveyed the info properly, so do you care to elaborate a bit further, Captain?

Capt. Valezquez: Well, other than the fact that Lieutenant Dooley was arrested and is now missing, there's really not much more to the story, Mr. Hogan.

Shawn: Did I hear you correctly, Captain? Did you just say that Lieutenant Dooley was missing?

Capt. Valezquez: Yes, you heard correctly, Mr. Hogan.

Shawn: I may not be a peritus when it comes to transporting prisoners, but how on earth does one come up missing while en route to jail, Captain?

Capt. Valezquez: Well, Mr. Hogan, I really don't have an explanation for this reviling situation because, even though I'm affiliated with the Jackson Police Department, I wasn't there when Lieutenant Dooley was abducted.

Shawn: Abducted?! I thought you said that he was missing, Captain, so you do know what happened to him. You know what, Captain Valezquez? At this point, I'm certain that my sister-in-law is most perturbed over the tragedy that has been intercalated into our lives. And though it is a rather abash moment for you and your department, this does not excuse the dubious ambivalence that we all share in regards to your chief's actions.

Capt. Valezquez: Mr. Hogan, to be honest, I'm not entirely understanding your language but I do understand and concur with you all's feelings, which is why Major Stephens and I will be working diligently, around the clock, to ensure that justice prevails for our friend and your brother-in-law.

Shawn: That's all we ask of you, Captain Valezquez. Now in retrospect, can you think of anything else you all could be overlooking here?

Capt. Valezquez: Well, Mr. Hogan, I think the only thing that I may have overlooked is the fact that this whole ordeal was probably planned from the get go. Therefore, I feel somewhat responsible for the abduction because, had I followed in persuit, I may have been able to prevent Lieutenant Dooley's dissappearance.

Shawn: Alright, good enough, sir. Since that is out of the question, then I feel that our next move should be to locate Lieutenant Dooley's whereabouts. And I'm certain Captain that you are aware, that time is of the essence.

Capt. Valezquez: Yes, I realize the urgency of Lieutenant Dooley's discovery, which is why I'm going to have to cut this conversation short and get back to work.

Shawn: Of course, I understand. Good luck to you, Captain Valezquez, and please forgive my line of questioning; I didn't mean it to be ill toward you. However, we do want to make this priority. wouldn't you agree?

Capt. Valezquez: Without a doubt; it's at the pinnacle of my duties. But again, Mr. Hogan, I do have to be going; no offense. Please give Mrs. Dooley and the rest of the family my regards, and I will keep you all informed of my progression in the matter.

(They both say goodbye and hang up. Captain Valezquez is now receiving a call from Sergeant Willansby . . .)

Capt. Valezquez: *(answering)* Hello? Captain Valezquez here.

Serg. Willansby: Yes hello, Captain Valezquez, this is Sergeant Willansby. I was calling to see what's going on. A few minutes ago, I got a call from Major Stephens and she notified me of Lieutenant Dooley's abduction; tell me it's not true.

Capt. Valezquez: Unfortunately Sergeant Willansby, it is true, and it's rumored that your favorite criminal, Money Mike, is one of the perps.

Serg. Willansby: Somehow, I'm not surprised to hear that Money Mike is involved. I also think that our boss is involved in this shenanigan, but I think we're in luck.

Capt. Valezquez: Luck? Yeah, we can use a bit of that at this point. Now what is it?

Serg. Willansby: Well Dennis, do you remember the last time I talked to you? I said that I needed to make a few calls.

Capt. Valezquez: Yeah, so what about it?

Serg. Willansby: It paid off some big dividends. I have a friend who happens to work the streets and, well, he has two sons who he just found out have been dealing with a guy named Black. Black happens to be his sobriquet; his forename is Jeremy Grayson. As luck would have it, he's Money Mike's right hand man.

Capt. Valezquez: Great news, Sweet Pea! Now what else do you have?

Serg. Willansby: What makes you think that I have more, Doughboy?

Capt. Valezquez: Your pertinacious character. I know that you would not have stopped there with your line of questioning, so come on, give up the goodies.

Serg. Willansby: Alright, I'm going to fill you in completely Dennis, but keep in mind, we have to be very discreet in our mission to rescue Lieutenant Dooley.

Capt. Valezquez: Yes, without a doubt, Sweet Pea. Now enough with the procrastination.

Serg. Willansby: Okay this guy, my associate, became my eyes and ears a few years ago, after I aborted his arrest and decided not to turn him in for prosecution. His name is John Allen Sanchez. One of his sons is a junior, and the other's name is Michael. John, Jr. just so happened to over hear Money Mike and his underling, Black, discussing Lieutenant Dooley's abduction. John, Jr. told his big brother, Michael, who was acquainted with Lieutenant Dooley by way of a guy named Marvin Robinson. In brief, Marvin and Michael got the information to John Sanchez, Sr. who, in turn, got the info to me.

Capt. Valezquez: So what made the two young fellas contact this Sanchez guy?

Serg. Willansby: As I said, one of them, Michael, is his son. However, they don't seem to have a good relationship. The other guy, Marvin, had already been cooperating with Lieutenant Dooley to investigate the absence of another young boy, Jimmy Nuttingham, who goes by the alias "June Bug". June Bug and John, Jr. are friends but, according to Michael, I'm not sure if June Bug is trustworthy. Anyhow, the point is, Lieutenant Dooley is said to be at their hideout, being tortured severely.

Capt. Valezquez: What?! Then what are we waiting for, Sergeant Willansby? Shouldn't we be raiding the place and rescuing Lieutenant Dooley?

Serg. Willansby: The impediment is a plan, Captain. We can't just go over there half cocked; we have to sort this thing out strategically. As a swat commander you, of all people, should know this, Dennis.

Capt. Valezquez: Yeah, you're right, Sweet Pea; I guess I let my emotions get the best of me. However, we're wasting imperative time. Does Major Stephens know about this yet, Sergeant Willansby?

Serg. Willansby: No, not just yet. Are you absolutely sure that she can be trusted, Dennis?

Capt. Valezquez: Most certainly; you have my word on it. Officer Lansing and Sergeant Johnson are also with us one hundred percent, and they need to be brought in on this as well.

Serg. Willansby: Yeah, we're going to need all the help that we can get, so let's see now . . . There's me, you, Major Stephens, Officer Lansing, and Sergeant Johnson. Is there anyone else we can use for this tactical maneuver, Dennis?

Capt. Valezquez: Yes, Sweet Pea, we can count on my entire command squad.

Serg. Willansby: Really? The whole SWAT force can be trusted?

Capt. Valezquez: Yes, absolutely. As a matter of fact, I'll call them all right now.

Serg. Willansby: Remember Dennis, discretion.

Capt. Valezquez: Roger that.

Serg. Willansby: I have a couple other comrades I can count on; I'll get hold of them. Let's all meet behind the old Sack-n-Save grocery store, over on North Side Boulevard, within the next hour, Dennis.

Capt. Valezquez: Copy that; I'm on it.

(They hang up and begin to act in relations to the phone call. Meanwhile, back at the Dooley's residence, Shawn is about to address Lillian and Kellie about the situation . . .)

Shawn: Lillian, my dear, I must confess that this matter has dilated much more than I expected.

Mrs. Dooley: *(murmuring in hysteria)* Yeah, I know, and if things keep going the way they're going, we'll be extirpated.

(Mrs. Dooley starts to cry. After observing, Kellie walks over to comfort Lillian.)

Kellie: There, there sis. It's going to be alright, just have faith.

Shawn: I'm sorry, Lillian, that was very flippant of me and I feel like a pedant for saying such a thing. Please forgive me for speaking out of character.

Mrs. Dooley: Oh, that's okay, Shawn; there's no apology needed. You were only stating the obvious. Things have gotten a little raveled to say the least.

Shawn: Well, don't worry, Lillian. Our collocation will eventually raze the matter and, if God's will, cause Lieutenant Dooley's preposterous chief to recant the charges.

Kellie: That would be like asking Satan himself to recant his actions, and we know that won't happen.

Mrs. Dooley: Don't be so pessimistic, Kellie. Anything is possible with God.

Kellie: Yeah, you're right Lillian, and I believe it's going to take a supernatural intervention for this thing to work out in our favor.

Shawn: Alright you all, enough of this reciprocating conversation. For now, let's put this matter aside and join the children in the kitchen. I'm eager to see my little man and my favorite niece and nephew. Besides, I'm famished. What have you to eat, Lillian? (On that note, everyone exits toward the kitchen . . .

In the interim, Sergeant Willansby and Captain Valezquez are awaiting the other officers at the appointed location {behind the old Sack-n-Save grocery store}.)

Serg. Willansby: *(talking to Captain Valezquez)* Hello again, Dennis. Have you contacted the rest of the crew?

Capt. Valezquez: Hello to you, Sweet Pea and yes, the fellas should be pulling up any minute now. Major Stephens will be with them.

Serg. Willansby: Great. I talked with Officer Lansing, Sergeant Johnson, and Corporal Davenport. I told them to meet here at six and it's about five forty-five now, so they should all be on their way. What's your strategy for this operation, Dennis?

Capt. Valezquez: Well, first off, I'm calling this "Operation Hush", for obvious reasons. Now here's the plan, Sweet Pea: I want you to get hold of your informant, uh . . . uh, what's his name?

Serg. Willansby: Sanchez. I know where you're going with this, and I'm way ahead of you. I talked with him a few minutes ago, and he's on standby as we speak. He's waiting with his son, Michael.

Michael has gotten hold of John Jr., who is at Money Mike's hideout now.

Capt. Valezquez: Good job, Sweet Pea. Remember when you first left the academy? I told you that you belonged with our tactical unit. Do you know if John Jr. spotted the lieutenant there at the location?

Serg. Willansby: As a matter of fact, I think he did mention something about Lieutenant Dooley being in a shed out back.

Capt. Valezquez: So you're not certain? We don't need dubiety dear, and we definitely don't want to run the risk of anyone getting hurt so if it's possible, we need to get John Jr. to corroborate Lieutenant Dooley's position.

Serg. Willansby: Okay, I'm on it. Give me a few minutes and hopefully, I should have that info for you.

(As they speak, the tactical SWAT unit arrives with Major Stephens, Sergeant Johnson and Officer Lansing. The only one absent is Corporal Davenport. Major Stephens gets out of her patrol car and walks over to Captain Valezquez, who is now standing with his tactical unit . . .)

Maj. Stephens: Hello, Captain Valezquez, how's it going? Is everything in order?

Capt. Valezquez: Hi ma'am. We're not completely set up here but we're working on it. Give me a minute and I'll fill you in, okay?

(Corporal Davenport finally arrives, accounting for all persons involved in the ensuing raid. She steps out of her car and, about five seconds later, several black SUV's pull up. Multiple FBI agents exit the vehicles, all wearing buttoned down suits. They have their weapons drawn and are ordering everyone to stay put. The head agent is one of the last to exit an SUV . . .)

FBI Agent: *(steps out and joins everyone in the corral)* Who's in charge here?

(Being the highest ranking officer, Major Stephens addresses the questioning agent . . .)

Maj. Stephens: I am, sir. I'm Major Stephens, but who are you and what's going on here?

FBI Agent: (flashes his badge and shakes Major Stephens' hand) I'm FBI agent, Melvin Archie ma'am, and we're here under the order of the United States' attorney general's office, by way of Governor Hatchetson. (Governor Hatchetson is the governor of Mississippi, where the event is taking place.)

Maj. Stephens: (now has a look of surprise and vivacity) Governor Hatchetson?! The attorney general?! What on earth is going on here Agent um . . . um . . . What did you say your name was?

FBI Agent: Agent Archie ma'am, and we're here to prevent the foray that you're planning because this raid could impair our ongoing investigation.

Maj. Stephens: And what, may I ask, is that investigation?

Agent Archie: I'm sorry ma'am, but I am not at liberty to disclose that information at this time. However, I will say this much: We know about your man, Lieutenant Dooley, and his abduction. We also know about the culprit, Money Mike.

Maj. Stephens: What?! Well, if you know all this, then why aren't you all at the location, rescuing him instead of regulating and harassing us?

Agent Archie: Because we have bigger fish to catch and, sorry to say, but since Lieutenant Dooley stuck his nose where it didn't belong, he's going to have to be the bait.

(After hearing that statement, Sergeant Willansby and Captain Valezquez spring forward in an attempt to assault Agent Archie, only to be intercepted by other agents . . .)

Serg. Willansby: How does taking care of business make an officer nosy? Who the hell are you to make such an accusation?

Agent Archie: I'm the H.N.I.C, despite your disbelief, and if you don't control yourself, I'll have you incarcerated. You wouldn't want to be locked up again, now would you, Sergeant?

(Referring to Sergeant Willansby's abduction, when she was locked in a room. Sergeant Willansby is astounded and infuriated by the agent's knowledge of this and is now wondering what the big picture is . . .)

Maj. Stephens: *(reaching out to Sergeant Willansby to pacify her)* Okay, settle down Sergeant, that's an order.

Agent Archie: If you would all calm down, I'll explain the situation in a more refined way.

(While Agent Archie speaks, Sergeant Willansby gets a call from Sanchez {the informant} in regards to Lieutenant Dooley's whereabouts. She answers the phone . . .)

Serg. Willansby: Hello? Sergeant Willansby here.

Sanchez: *(panicked)* Sergeant Willansby! Sergeant Willansby, ya'll gotta hurry! They're beating him up; you gotta hu . . .

Serg. Willansby: *(interrupting Sanchez)* Hold on, Sanchez; slow down a minute. Now what's going on, and who's beating who?

Sanchez: *(catches his breath and gains composure)* Okay, I'm calm but Sergeant, if ya'll don't hurry up and get over there, they're gonna kill him.

Serg. Willansby: Who are you talking about, Sanchez? *(Trying to discern whether Sanchez is referring to his son or the lieutenant)*

Sanchez: *(yelling)* Lieutenant Dooley; I'm talking about Lieutenant Dooley! Michael told me that John, Jr. mentioned seeing Black, Money Mike, and a couple other guys drag Lieutenant Dooley out, and that Money Mike had kicked Lieutenant Dooley in the chest. So if he's not already dead, ya'll better hurry up and get over there now.

(Now, with mixed feelings of hysteria, fear and animation, Sergeant Willansby turns to Captain Valezquez and Major Stephens . . .)

Serg. Willansby: Captain! Major! That was my informant, Sanchez, on the phone. He just told me that they are over there, beating Lieutenant Dooley right now. We need to move on this expeditiously.

Capt. Valezquez: What?! Oh no! I promised Mrs. Dooley that I would look after the lieutenant. Major Stephens, we gotta do something here, ma'am. It's your call; do we sit here and argue with these agents or do we get there and rescue a fellow officer?

Maj. Stephens: *(turns to the agent in charge)* Did you hear what my officers just said, Agent Archie? We have an officer down and his life is in peril. Now what do you suggest we do?

(Agent Archie pauses, as to decide if he should allow them to act on the given information. Unhappy with Agent Archie's sluggish response, Sergeant Willansby abruptly pulls her revolver, walks over to Agent Archie, and puts it to his head. Agent Archie's auxiliary agents ready their weapons. Notwithstanding, Sergeant Willansby stands her ground . . .)

Serg. Willansby: Let Captain Valezquez and the rest of the crew leave now, or the FBI is going to be one agent short.

Maj. Stephens: Sergeant Willansby, please stand down; this is not the way to handle this.

Serg. Willansby: Oh yeah? Well, I don't see any other way, Major and besides, we don't have time to debate here. My friend and partner has been abducted and is possibly being killed right now, and ya'll gonna stand here with this bureaucratic flim flam? Well I'm sorry, Lieutenant Dooley has a family and he deserves better than what's going on here. So what's it gonna be? *(Still aiming the cocked weapon at Agent Archie)* One . . . Two . . .

Agent Archie: Alright, alright . . . *(Turns his attention to his men)* Stand down and let them go, guys.

(Returns his attention to Sergeant Willansby) Now understand this, Sergeant: I'm still in charge here and I will be leading this mission, like it or not, so when we get to your lieutenant's alleged location, I want my main three men: agents Gerod, Styles, and Chan to handle this Money Mike character. As ex military special forces, they are more physically ready to subdue this guy. And as for you, Sergeant Willansby, I will attend to you later.

Serg. Willansby: *(angrily and sarcastically responds)* Oh whatever, Agent Orange, do what you have to; I did.

(Sergeant Willansby and the others holster their weapons and head for their vehicles. After everyone enters their vehicles, Sergeant Willansby leads them to Money Mike's hideout . . . Ten minutes later, they arrive at the scene. It's twilight and everyone is assembled within spitting distance of the perimeter. They are now receiving instructions from FBI agent, Archie . . .)

Agent Archie: Alright people, here's the deal: I want you *(pointing at Agent Manuel and Agent Duegen)* to head out as F.O.'s *(Forward Observers)*. Once you all pinpoint Lieutenant Dooley and Money Mike's location, radio me and I'll send in agents Styles, Chan and Gerod, who will then rush in and apprehend the perp. Everyone else will close in the perimeter, conquering the rest of the culprits as we go. Now remember, if possible, take Money Mike alive but if it's a matter of your life and his, do what you gotta do, understood? Okay, is everybody ready to move out?

(Everyone nods in agreement. Agent Archie then motions for his main three agents to move out, and for everybody else to wait for his command. Meanwhile, inside of Money Mike's hideout is his counter part, Black, along with three other guys. Sanchez's son {John, Jr.}, Little Jimmy, and two other young boys {who were selling guns out of back packs in conjunction with Black} are also inside the building . . . Unfortunately, Sergeant Willansby and the others are not aware that these kids are in the building, so this may hamper the operation. Agent Archie has just ordered the F.O.'s to move out . . .)

(Agents Duegen, Manuel, and Chan are now in their assigned positions. Agent Chan is about to radio Agent Archie with reference to his sight of Money Mike.)

Agent Chan: *(speaking in code)* F.O. Chan to Agent Archie; I have located the cat. He has the rat in his paw as we speak.

Agent Archie: Roger that, F.O. Chan. Hold your position but continue to observe until I sanction you to capture the pole cat.

Agent Chan: Copy that, Commander.

Agent Archie: *(speaking to everybody back at the holdup camp)* Agent Chan has spotted Money Mike alone with Lieutenant Dooley. Now on a count of three, I want everyone to move out and do as they were instructed . . . One . . . Two . . . Three, Go!

(The incursion is in motion. The three focal agents are about to march into Money Mike's lair in attempt to rescue Mr. Dooley. They kick in the door and rush in. Instantaneously, Money Mike jumps to his feet. They all order him to freeze and to put his hands on top of his head, ignorant of the fact that Money Mike only obeys Dr. Elenski. Money Mike starts

walking toward agents Chan and Duegen, so they order him to stop again but he disregards, forcing them to open fire. {They don't want to wrestle with him because Money Mike is huge, about 6' 8" and 350 pounds.} Improbably, the borage of bullets does not hinder him. Agent Chan walks up to Money Mike and does a round house kick to his face, but that does not hurt him by any means. In actual fact, it only provokes him. He picks Agent Duegen up off the floor, raises him over his head, and launches him at Agent Chan. Subsequently, Agent Manuel creeps up behind him with an extended assault baton. He swings and hits Money Mike in the head, not once but twice, so Money Mike gyrates and walks toward Agent Manuel. Agent Manuel begins to retreat, at what time agents Chan and Duegen get back on their feet. As they advance to assist Agent Manuel, Sergeant Willansby, Captain Valezquez and two other officers enter the room. Sergeant Willansby browses the room and notices Lieutenant Dooley slumped over in a corner, covered in blood. As she rushes to his aid, the others are trying to help the agents subdue Money Mike. However, they are not doing a very good job. By design, Money Mike is throwing them all around like rag dolls. Sergeant Willansby is now cradling Mr. Dooley in her lap, with tears in her eyes . . .)

Serg. Willansby: *(gazes into Mr. Dooley's eyes, hoping that he will open them)* Jonathan . . . Jonathan . . .

Come on, wake up. Jonathan, wake up . . . Please, for God's sake, wake up. We need you; don't you give up on us. I'm here for you. It's me, Sweet Pea. Please get up, Jonathan . . .

(There's still no response, so Sergeant Willansby directs her attention to her fellow officers, who are boisterously and ineffectively struggling to apprehend Money Mike. Triggered by her compassion for Mr. Dooley, Sergeant Willansby draws her revolver {a forty-five} and walks over to the others, demanding them to get out of her way. Everyone is at a stand-still and all eyes are on her. They all back away as Sergeant Willansby aims her gun at Money Mike.)

Serg. Willansby: *(yelling)* I hope you have things right with your maker, Money Mike, because you are about to visit him.

Money Mike: *(looks at her and laughs aloud)* You know, it's funny you should say that because, fortunately, I do have things right with him. As a matter of fact, I met with him just a little while ago.

(The spectators aren't aware that he is referring to his earthly maker, Dr. Elenski, so they look at each other as if to say, "What on earth is he talking about? This guy is a lunatic." . . .)

Serg. Willansby: Well good, then he shouldn't mind you coming back to see him. *(She opens fire on him.)*

Agent Chan: Hold your fire, Sergeant; it won't do you any good. We already tried that, and he wouldn't go down. *(Now everyone in the room is in awe.)*

Money Mike: Good luck saving your lieutenant's life, people.

(Money Mike turns and runs out of the room. On the way out, he knocks Agent Archie and a couple others down. Thus, generating another successful getaway. Agent Archie gets to his feet and asks . . .)

Agent Archie: What was that?

Capt. Valezquez: That, Agent Archie, was your perp. You know, the one you said your fantastic three were more physically ready to handle. I mean, correct me if I'm wrong fellas, but when we came on the scene, they didn't seem so fantastic to me.

(All three agents hang their heads in shame.)

Agent Archie: I can't believe my ears! One guy overtook three former special forces?!

Agent Manuel: But sir, that wasn't no ordinary guy; he had the strength of ten men.

Agent Archie: *(cynically responds)* Oh, now I know I'm dreaming because, in real life, an ex green beret would never have had trouble with one individual.

Agent Duegen: *(also speaking in their defense)* But sir, he's telling you the truth. That guy was not your average perp. All I can say is, you'd have to see it to believe it.

Serg. Willansby: Why are you all wasting time, trying to justify yourselves for this nit-picker? He had just as much of a chance to apprehend the guy as you all did. Hell, he ran right pass him and three other agents, didn't he? *(All three agents nod conformably)* Okay, then why? Explain.

Capt. Valezquez: Yeah, Agent Archie, tell us why you all didn't seize that "one guy", who knocked you all over on his way to freedom.

Agent Archie: *(stuttering)* Because I . . . I . . . I didn't know who he . . . but he was too fa . . . fast, so how could I grab hold of him?

Serg. Willansby: Yeah right, and that's why we didn't get him either then, because he was too fast and we didn't know him, sir.

(Although it isn't a laughing matter, everyone guffaws. Major Stephens, Sergeant Johnson and Officer Lansing walk in on the laughter . . .)

Maj. Stephens: What's going on here that's so hilarious? I hope it's a celebration of Lieutenant Dooley's safe rescue and the apprehension of his perp.

Serg. Willansby: No ma'am, unfortunately, it's not. To tell the truth, I almost forgot.

(She turns and runs back over to Mr. Dooley.)

Maj. Stephens: *(joins Sergeant Willansby at Mr. Dooley's side)* Sergeant Willansby, what happened? Is he alright?

Serg. Willansby: No, he's non-responsive and needs medical attention ASAP.

Maj. Stephens: Quick, someone call 911 and get an ambulance here stat.

(Officer Lansing gets on his radio and calls for an ambulance. All the other culprits have been captured, and everyone is round up. Out of the blue, a jangle comes from the closet in the very room that everyone is in. Alarmed, the officers instantly pull their weapons and focus on the closet . . .)

Agent Archie: I advise whoever is in there to come out with their hands up, or we will start blasting through the door.

(Immediately after Agent Archie's caveat, the sound of crying comes from the door. Indistinct voices of fearful children exclaim, "Please don't shoot! Please don't shoot us; we're coming out!" Four little boys exit the closet. They are Little Jimmy, John Jr., and two others who are anonymous. When they walk out, they are ordered to keep their hands on top of their heads. Now Agent Archie is about to speak to them . . .)

Agent Archie: *(criticizing the young boys as they come out in single file)* Well, well, well . . . Now what do we have here? A closet full of diminutive criminals, perhaps?

Serg. Willasnby: Come on now, Agent Archie, you ought to be ashamed of yourself, convicting these kids before we have a chance to ascertain their reason for being here.

Agent Archie: Alright Sergeant, you have a point; let's just see if I jumped the gun in my indictment. Okay boys, why were you all hiding here in the closet and, more specifically, what are you doing here with a criminal as notorious and diabolical as Money Mike?

(All the boys start to explain in chorus, which makes it impractical for anyone to distinguish what they are saying. The boys are still in dread from all the ruckus that occurred just moments ago.)

Maj. Stephens: *(walks over to a couple of the boys and puts her arms around them)* Calm down, guys. It's okay, we're not going to hurt you. We just wanna know your names and why you all were here, okay? Now let's start with you, young man (looking at one of the boys in her arms).

(The boy commences to talk. Still edgy, he speaks rather faintly . . .)

First Boy: My name is John Sanchez, Jr. and the reason we are here is uh . . . uh . . .

(Seeing that John is nervous and doesn't know what to say, another one of the four boys speaks out . . .)

Second Boy: Alright, ya'll; I'll tell ya'll why we're here.

Maj. Stephens: Okay, little brave one. And, if you don't mind me asking, who are you?

Second Boy: Oh yeah, I'm Little Jimmy, AKA June Bug.

Maj. Stephens: Well, Little Bug or whatever you call yourself, is that your real name?

Little Jimmy: Nah, that's just what they call me on the streets. My granny calls me Jimmy.

Maj. Stephens: Alright then, Jimmy, do you have a last name?

Little Jimmy: Duh! Everybody has a last name.

(Everyone starts to laugh, including Major Stephens.)

Maj. Stephens: Good, I'm glad to hear that you know this. Now would you care to tell us yours?

Little Jimmy: Well, if you just gotta know it, my name is Jimmy Nuttingham. *(Sergeant Willansby recognizes his last name from an incident that Mr. Dooley told her about, so she cuts in . . .)*

Serg. Willansby: So you're Little Jimmy, huh? I finally get to meet you.

Agent Archie: Alright, enough of this reunion or whatever it may be. Can someone enlighten me of what's going on here?

Maj. Stephens: Yeah, me too. I'm curious as to how this little fella, Lieutenant Dooley, and Money Mike connect.

Serg. Willansby: Okay, I'll try to make this as brief as I can . . . Well, this little guy here (pointing at Little Jimmy) was presumably a friend to Little Jay; that's Lieutenant Dooley's son. However, something was going on between the two young men and, to sort it out, Lieutenant Dooley paid Little Jimmy's granny a visit. In turn, she told him where Little Jimmy hung out, which is at the M & M Pool Hall. That's where Lieutenant Dooley got acquainted with Money Mike. They got into a brawl and Lieutenant Dooley called for backup. Officer Lansing and I were part of the entourage that showed up to back him. Anyhow, this is the little guy Lieutenant Dooley was seeking, to return him to his granny.

Agent Archie: So you're telling me that Lieutenant Dooley was tracking Money Mike to find this one little guy?

Serg. Willansby: No, you idiot; that report was only to incorporate Little Jimmy into the equation. I won't discuss the other issue of his investigation because it's classified and ongoing.

Agent Archie: Ongoing?! The way things look with Lieutenant Dooley, I doubt if anything will be ongoing.

(Once again, Agent Archie's lackadaisical attitude frustrates Sergeant Willansby, so she lashes out to attack him but is cut off by Captain Valezquez and Agent Manuel.)

Serg. Willansby: I'm not going to tolerate your insolence toward Lieutenant Dooley, especially after he has been hurt while trying to do his job.

Agent Archie: Job?! You call hounding an adolescent fugitive who doesn't want to go home a job Sergeant? Shouldn't a patrol cop handle such a trivial circumstance, rather than a homicide Lieutenant? (Sergeant Willansby is now yelling obscenities.)

Maj. Stephens: Alright! Alright! Now both of you, stop all this dissipation. Can't you all see that there are kids present? Now I don't know about you all, but I'm ready to go catch that tyrant who just assaulted a number of federal agents and policemen, and don't overlook the fact that Lieutenant Dooley might not make it. So let's put this personal exacerbation behind and tend to our utmost concern; that is, if you can be compatible enough to do so.

Serg. Willansby: Yeah, you're right Major Stephens; I'm sorry for losing my head. Let's get out of here before I do something that I won't regret. (Though angry, being sarcastic).

Agent Archie: (responding to her sarcastic remark) Yes, let's do that, because we wouldn't want another policeman going to the hospital, now would we?

Agent Chan: No disrespect sir, but it's very awry and anomalous for a commanding FBI agent to be conducting himself like this, wouldn't you say?

(Everyone quiets down and centers their attention on Agent Archie, waiting for his response.)

Agent Archie: (looking sternly at Agent Chan) Agent Chan, I'm not even going to try to decipher what that statement meant. Let's just go for now, and while you're trying to tell me how to do my job, round up Little Jimmy, John Jr., and the other two hooligans. Take them over to J.P.D.'S juvenile division for further questioning . . . And I hope you can handle them better than you did Money Mike.

Maj. Stephens: What about the others? (Referring to Black and three other guys who were with Money Mike)

Agent Archie: Take them all to jail and hold them until I get back with you.

(Everyone exits the building and gets into their vehicles. Captain Valezquez gets on the phone to call Mrs. Dooley but after deciding that it would be better to tell her the bad news in person, he quickly hangs up. Meanwhile, back at the Dooleys' residence, everyone is sitting at the table, eating the meal that Kellie prepared . . .)

Shawn: (commending Kellie for her culinary skills) Well, I must say, you haven't lost your touch in the kitchen, Kellie.

Kellie: Why thanks for the compliment, Shawn, but did you think that I would just because you weren't around? Mark and I still had to eat.

Mrs. Dooley: Alright Kellie, please don't instigate. He gave you a compliment; take it in stride.

(Mark also interjects and defends his dad . . .)

Mark: Yeah ma. Why do you have to criticize dad's compliments all the time? Don't you want him to say good things about you, or is it that you are still mad at him for what he did such a long time ago?

Kellie: No baby, it's not that mom doesn't want your dad to say good things; mom just wants him to be good, too.

Mark: But mom, in Sunday school, they taught me that there are no good people, not one. Only God is good, so unless the bible is a lie, how can dad or any of us be good?

Kellie: Nothing in the bible is a lie son, and don't you ever forget that, but as you get older, you will better understand what that particular passage of scripture meant. We, as individuals, are not good by nature but with Christ living in us, we can become good. For we can do all things through Jesus Christ.

Mark: So then, are you are saying that dad doesn't have Jesus in his life?

(Kellie is tentative of how to respond to Mark's question. For Shawn has just recently conveyed his acceptance of Christ to her and Lillian, so she kind of trips over her tongue . . .)

Kellie: No, I'm saying that . . . I mean, he . . . Well, if he had Christ, uh . . . Well, he would not have . . .

Mrs. Dooley: Now Kellie, you need to stop with all that stuttering and just acknowledge that Shawn has accepted the Lord as his Savior now. Put the past behind you once and for all.

Diamerald: Yeah, Auntie Kellie, you might as well give up and leave Uncle Shawn alone, 'cause you know that Mark and Little Jay don't like nobody talking about their daddies.

Mrs. Dooley: Excuse me for butting in Diamerald, but are'nt you the same way younglady?

Diamerald: No I'm not; well at least not to the extent that they are.

Kellie: Yeah right, girl! Don't you remember the time when we were at the park, and some guy started hitting on your mom? When you looked over and saw what was going on, you ran over there like a speeding bullet, just to tell the guy that your mom was spoken for. You also told him that she loved your dad very much. I felt so bad for the poor guy that I wanted to give him my phone number.

(Everybody starts laughing, except Mark.)

Mark: Really mom? You wanted to give another guy your phone number? Maybe that's why dad did what he did, then.

Shawn: No son, your mom was just kidding . . . I guess. No, I'm joking. Your mom was and still is a very faithful and beautiful woman. It was I who messed things up.

Kellie: Flattery will get you nowhere dear, but thanks for the compliment anyway.

Mrs. Dooley: Girl, you so crazy.

Diamerald: You sure are, auntie. I need to hang around you more often; then I'd know how to turn guys away.

Mrs. Dooley: Just what do you mean by that, young lady?

Little Jay: She means just that, mom. She needs to be taught how to just say no to guys.

Diamerald: Well, at least I don't need a lesson in saying no to drugs, you little pea brain.

Mrs. Dooley: What?! Are you doing drugs, Little Jay?

Little Jay: No, ma'am! . . . See there, stupid, now you got mom thinking I'm a drug addict or something.

Diamerald: And you got her thinking that I'm a slut or something; so there, now we're even.

Kellie: Alright, hold it you two, enough of all that name calling and stuff.

Mark: See there, mom, that's how you and dad look when ya'll do it.

Kellie: But we are adults.

Shawn: That doesn't make it right. Honey, our son has a valid point; let's just try and take heed.

(While Shawn is speaking, Officer Douglas comes in to notify Mrs. Dooley that she has another visitor. It's Captain Valezquez, who is now entering the house. Mrs. Dooley follows close behind Officer Douglas, along with everyone else. After seeing Captain Valezquez, Mrs. Dooley's countenance is enveloped with panic because she is inquisitive of his purpose for coming . . .)

Mrs. Dooley: Hi there, Captain Valezquez, what brings you here?

Capt. Valezquez: (seeing the kids present, he is reluctant to speak) Hello to you all. I'm here on business. (looking at Shawn) Is this your brother-in-law?

Mrs. Dooley: Yes it is. Now what business are you here on, Captain?

Capt. Valezquez: Can we go somewhere private to converse, Mrs. Dooley? I don't think the kids need to take part in this conversation. (Diamerald is quick-witted enough to perceive that something is amiss, so she speaks out . . .)

Diamerald: Why not, Captain Valezquez? Is it because something has happened to my dad?

Little Jay: Dad?! Something has happened to dad?!

Mrs. Dooley: No son, nothing has happened to your dad. Right, Captain Valezquez?

Capt. Valezquez: Please, Mrs. Dooley, not in front of the kids.

Shawn: Yeah Lillian, I agree with the captain. Let's excuse the kids, okay?

Mrs. Dooley: (yelling) No, I'm done hiding the truth from my babies, so you might as well tell me what you gotta say right now, Captain!

Kellie: Okay Lillian, calm down. Maybe we should excuse the children.

Mrs. Dooley: (with tears in her eyes) Oh, so now the truth doesn't matter to you either, huh Kellie? Aren't you the one who's always saying it will set us free? Well, I need to be set free from all this stress right now. Is that okay with you?

Kellie: Yeah, you're right, Lillian. Okay Captain, why don't you go ahead and tell all of us what's going on?

Capt. Valezquez: Alright then. Well, we did locate Lieutenant Dooley, but he has been hurt very badly.

(Everyone starts to talk all at once, questioning the captain about what happened. Up till now, the kids never knew that Mr. Dooley was arrested or missing, so they're even more baffled about what has just been said. Shawn is now trying to calm everyone down, so that they can hear the entire account . . .)

Shawn: Okay everyone, please lets calm down here and let Captain Valezquez finish clarifying what happened.

Capt. Valezquez: As I was saying, we did find where the lieutenant was being held but, unfortunately, we didn't get there in time to stop the perps from harming him.

Mrs. Dooley: (with Little Jay and Diamerald both huddled in her arms) Captain Valezquez, all I want to know is where Jonathan is right now.

Capt. Valezquez: An ambulance has taken him to St. Mary's Hospital. Actually, he should be there by now.

(Diamerald, Little Jay, and Mark all ask Mrs. Dooley about the clandestine affair that has been going on behind their backs and she sheds light on everything, bringing them up to speed. Now everyone is preparing to go to the hospital . . .)

(Everyone arrives at St. Mary's Hospital and files into the building. The Dooley family is now at the entrance of the emergency room, being met by Major Stephens and Sergeant Willansby . . .)

Serg. Willansby: Hi there, Lillian. How have you and the kids been getting along, especially with all that has transpired in the last few weeks?

Mrs. Dooley: Hello to you, Sergeant Willansby, and thanks for your concern but to be perfectly honest, my life has been nightmarish since the beginning of Jonathan's tribulation, so much so that I even dared to tell Diamerald and Little Jay what was going on.

Serg. Willansby: Oh my God, Lillian! Are you telling me that Diamerald and Little Jay didn't know what happened to their dad?! And today, when they do find out, he's lying here in the hospital, fighting for his life.

Mrs. Dooley: What?! Fighting for his life?! Sergeant Willansby, is it really that serious? (She starts to cry.)

Serg. Willansby: (embraces Mrs. Dooley to console her in her flaccidity) There there, darling. It's going to be alright; you and I both know that Jonathan is a perseverant man.

(Captain Valezquez and Kellie walk over as Sergeant Willansby consoles Mrs. Dooley. Kellie begins to comfort Mrs. Dooley in place of Sergeant Willansby, who is now scolding Captain Valezquez for having not informing Mrs. Dooley of her husbands condition as they walk away from Kellie and Mrs. Dooley).

Serg. Willansby: Dennis, why didn't you tell me that you hadn't informed Mrs. Dooley of Jonathan's condition? I just blabbered out to her that he was fighting for dear life.

Capt. Valezquez: Oh, I'm sorry, but it wasn't due to a lack of effort on my part. I tried to tell her and she told me that all she wanted to know was where her husband was, so of course, I wasn't going to divulge any more information than that.

(Captain Valezquez and Sergeant Willansby's conversation is interrupted with a loud commotion of arguing. Mrs. Dooley and Diamerald are at the receptionist's desk, demanding to see Mr. Dooley, while Kellie, Shawn, and Major Stephens are trying to pacify the situation . . .)

Diamerald: (yelling) I wanna see my daddy; I wanna see him right now! . . . Why can't I see him, huh? Why won't ya'll let me see my daddy?

Mrs. Dooley: (also getting very irate, while crying and yelling) Please, just let me see him! I need to see Jonathan! . . . Please Shawn, make them let me see my husband.

Shawn: Okay Lillian, I hear you and I will, but please settle down. I promise you, you will see Jonathan. Just give them a little time to help him feel better, alright?

(Due to their ages, Mark and Little Jay have been taken out, away from all the melee. Meanwhile, Sergeant Willansby is calling her daughter, Barbara, who just recently discovered that Mr. Dooley is her biological father. Mrs. Dooley, Diamerald, and Little Jay have yet to find out . . .)

Serg. Willansby: (speaking to Barbara) Hey, baby girl, what are you up to?

Barbara: Oh, hi mom, nothing much; just sitting here, trying to catch up on my studies. So what's up with you? Shouldn't you be at home, getting your rest?

Serg. Willansby: Oh, how I wish! Unfortunately, something came up.

Barbara: Now what could be more important than taking care of numeral uno, huh mom?

Serg. Willansby: Listen honey, I have some bad news.

Barbara: What?! Don't tell me those guys are after you again, ma! (Serg. Willansby just pause in her speech and holds the phone). Ma! What is it? Will you please stop procrastinating and tell me already.

Serg. Willansby: Okay! Okay Barbara, it's Lieutenant Dooley, dear.

Barbara: Oh no, please don't let it be true, Father God! Mom I had a bad dream about him just last night.

Serg. Willansby: Really?! What was the dream, Barbara?

Barbara: Never mind, mom, it was merely a dream. Just tell me what's going on in the real world, okay, please.

Serg. Willansby: (sighs) Alright. He has been beaten severely and is at the hospital right now, fighting for his life.

Barbara: What! In the hospital?! Mom which hospital is he at?

Serg. Willansby: St. Mary's, dear. I'm here now, along with the family.

Barbara: I'm on my way, mom. (They both hang up. Soon after, an ER doctor walks out and asks for the Dooley family's representative, so Shawn speaks up while awaiting Mrs. Dooley, Kellie and Diamerald, who are on their way in the direction as he . . .)

Shawn: Hello sir, we are here for Dooley. What's going on?

Doctor: Okay good, and who are you, may I ask?

Shawn: (While reaching out to shake the doctor's hand) I'm Lieutenant Dooley's brother-in-law, Shawn Hogan.

Doctor: Well, I am ER specialist, Dr. Shaderi. Are you the closest of kin here, Mr. Hogan?
(Before Shawn can respond, Mrs. Dooley, Kellie and Diamerald walk up.)

Mrs. Dooley: (responding to the doctor's question) No, he isn't, I am. I'm his wife and this (pointing) is our daughter, Diamerald. So what's going on Doctor . . . . ?

Dr. Shaderi: Shaderi, ma'am. (Reaches out to a chair as a gesture for her to be seated) I think you better have a seat, Mrs. Dooley.

Mrs. Dooley: No, I don't feel like sitting right now. Please, just tell me about my husband.

Dr. Shaderi: Alright, Mrs. Dooley, but do you want me to continue with your daughter present?

(Mrs. Dooley replies with, "Yes, it's okay." Simultaneously, Diamerald speaks for herself as well and says, "Yes, you can continue doctor, because I'm not leaving anyway.")

Dr. Shaderi: Okay, Mrs. Dooley and Diamerald, here's the diagnosis: I don't know if you all knew it or not, but Mr. Dooley was cataleptic when he was brought in here to us. He had internal hemorrhage, as well as lesions and contusions, a couple of fractured ribs, a major concussion and a spinal disjunction so, in hopes of avoiding paralysis, we had to stabilize him immediately. His right arm was pivoted, so much that his bone was detached. The retina in his right eye is irrevocably nucleated, and his femur was also broken.

(Mrs. Dooley, Diamerald, Kellie, Sergeant Willansby and Major Stephens are all tearful as Dr. Shaderi expounds the extent of Mr. Dooley's injuries.)

Dr. Shaderi: We are doing everything humanly possible to, not only save his life, but to preserve his body parts. But to be quite candid, people, it doesn't look too good right now; so if you all will excuse me, I need to get back into the operating room. I only came out to clarify Mr. Dooley's condition.

Shawn: We know and do thank you, Dr. Shaderi, for your explication. Is there anything we can do to expedite you all's efforts?

Dr. Shaderi: Yes. As a matter of fact, I'm glad you asked, because he's going to need a blood transfusion, so if you all would, get with my nurse so that she can direct you to the right location and see if any of you are compatible donors.

Shawn: Alright, we're on it. Anything else?

Dr. Shaderi: Yes, send up lots and lots of prayers, people because it's going to take a miracle for him to even make it through the night.

Kellie: I'm already on the line with Jesus, Dr. Shaderi. Thank you, and please don't let that man die in there; he's a good guy.

Dr. Shaderi: And if he wasn't a good guy, do you think that I would do any less of a job to save his life? I'm sorry ma'am, and I hope I don't sound mean spirited, but I do my best for all my patients, irregardless of their character.

Kellie: Yes, of course you do, Dr. Shaderi; please forgive me. I didn't mean it that way, I guess I let my emotions get the best of me because its personal.

Dr. Shaderi: I understand, and no apology is warranted, but I must be going.

(As he exits the room, two plain clothes men walk through the door of the emergency room. They are investigators from Internal Affairs. They both walk up and greet Major Stephens and Sergeant Willansby. One of them asks Major Stephens who she is . . .)

Maj. Stephens: I'm Major Stephens, and who are you?

(The investigator reaches into his jacket and pulls out his badge.)

Investigator: I am Investigator O'Hare, with Internal Affairs.

(The other investigator a black female by the name of Cheryl Keagan already knows Major Stephens because she has spoken with her before.)

Other investigator: Hello there, Major Stephens. Good to see you again, but I am contrite to have to see you at such a dismal period. Even so, it's an erratic duty, as you know. So with that being said, by orders of the attorney general's office, we are here to investigate the abduction of Lieutenant Jonathan Dooley, and your solidarity in this matter would be greatly appreciated.

Maj. Stephens: Yes of course, Investigator Keagen, but what is it that you need from me, ma'am?

(Investigator O'Hare speaks out to Major Stephens . . .)

Invest. O'Hare: Well first, we need to know who issued the warrant for Officer Dooley's arrest, and secondly, who arrested and transported the prisoner?

Serg. Willansby: (cantankerously interposing) Excuse you! Prisoner?! Lieutenant Dooley is not anyone's prisoner, mind you. He is an officer of the law being baselessly incriminated by his own boss, and I am discussed by your indecency, calling him a prisoner before he has even been tried.

Invest. O'Hare: And who are you, ma'am?

Serg. Willansby: I'm Sergeant Willansby, with the Jackson Police Department, and Lieutenant Dooley's former partner. I hope that you all are here to see that justice prevails.

Invest. O'Hare: That's exactly what we plan to do, so stay out of the way and let us do our job here, Sergeant, and if we need your advice, we will ask for it. Until then, keep your comments to yourself, okay?

(Now Sergeant Willansby has gotten even more irate and is about to let the investigator have it. Luckily, Major Stephens interrupts her and commands her to be at ease. Sergeant Willansby complies and sits down . . . Major Stephens is now speaking to the investigators.)

Maj. Stephens: Alright, Chief McClemens is the person who ordered the warrant for Lieutenant Dooley's arrest, and the two officers who were transporting him to jail were Officers Melvin Jordan and Corporal Jacelyn Davenport, all of whom are with J.P.D.

(Both investigators take notes as Major Stephens speaks. They then tell her that they will be back in touch if they needed to talk to her any further. Then they depart.)

(Barbara has just arrived at the hospital. Sergeant Willansby notices her coming through the door. She then turns to Major Stephens to let her know that her daughter has arrived. Major Stephens decides to go over and converse with Shawn Kellie's ex-husband, while Sergt. Willansby goes to greet her daughter).

Barbara: Hi there, mom, how are things going so far? Has the doctor said anything further about his condition yet?

Serg. Willansby: Yes baby, he did, and it didn't sound positive at all. As a matter of fact, he spelled out everything that those thugs did to Jonathan.

Barbara: Yeah? Well, what exactly did he say, mom?

Serg. Willansby: Honey, you don't wanna hear it.

Barbara: (yelling hysterically) Momma, will you please just tell me already?! For God's sake, I'm not a kid anymore! And besides, he is my dad; or did you forget again?

(Diamerald hears someone yelling, so she follows the voice. She looks near the entrance, where she spots Barbara standing with her mom. Realizing that it was Barbara yelling, Diamerald begins to wonder who she was referring to. For she overheard Barbara say something about someone being her dad, so Diamerald walks over to speak with Barbara and Sergeant Willansby . . .)

Diamerald: (with a look of suspicion) Hi Barbara, I thought that was you I heard over here; good to see you again. Is everything okay?

Barbara: (is now flabbergasted but tries to downplay the conversation) Yes, it's me girl, and it's good to see you too, but why did you ask me if everything was okay?

Diamerald: Well, primarily, because it sounded like you and your mom were arguing or having some sort of disagreement.

Barbara: What? Arguing with my mom? Oh no, I was just overwhelmed about Uncle Dooley's unfortunate situation.

(Diamerald doesn't believe that Sergeant Willansby has had a chance to tell Barbara about the situation.)

Diamerald: Well, did your mom fill you in on his condition?

Barbara: Yeah, she did, somewhat.

Diamerald: Okay good, and we're glad you cared enough to come by and show your support to the family.

Barbara: Now would you expect anything less of me, Diamerald? You know how I feel about my Uncle Dooley.

Diamerald: Yeah, I know, and I shouldn't be surprised to see you here in support of your own dad . . . Oh, my bad I mean Uncle Dooley.

(Diamerald purposely makes this statement to see how Barbara and Sergeant Willansby reacts. However, neither of them budge. Barbara is quick-witted and vindictive, so she decides to strike back.)

Barbara: Oh, that's okay girl, I understand how you could make such a mistake, because he did always treat me like his own child, didn't he? The only reason I call him uncle is out of respect to you and Little Jay, 'cause I know you guys love your dad too much to wanna share him.

(Sergeant Willansby gives Barbara a look, as if to say "Stop with those remarks.")

Diamerald: (now has an even more serious look on her face) Yeah, you got that right, because we don't need no feigned sibling coming out the woodwork some twenty years later, trying to fit in now that they think our dad is dying and hope to gain something from it. That ain't happening, so they might as well keep being who they were for the last twenty years, sister . . . and I don't mean that literally.

(Barbara and Diamerald are starting to get rather loud and unruly, so Mrs. Dooley and Kellie walk over to see what all the commotion is.)

Barbara: Did you say feigned?! Now what would make you think that this sibling who, as you put it, is coming out of the woodwork, is feigned? Who's to say that it's not your real sibling? And maybe they could care less about profiting from their dad's unfortunate circumstance, sister . . . and I do mean sister.

Diamerald: Well, if they were really our sibling and cared anything about us or our dad, they would've made it known long before now. Wouldn't you agree, Barbara? And I do mean Barbara.

Mrs. Dooley: (Mrs. Dooley and her sister Kellie walks over to investigate what appears to be an argument between Diamerald and Barbara). Hey, what's going on here? What on earth are you girls arguing about? You all are acting like sibling rivals. Now what's the problem here, Diamerald?

Serg. Willansby: Oh, it's nothing Lillian, they're just rehearsing a play; it's an assignment that they received in their drama class. Ain't that right, girls?

(Sergeant Willansby gives them both a supplicatory look, as if to say, "Please, don't tell Mrs. Dooley; this is not the time." Barbara and Diamerald both relent and say . . .)

Barbara and Diamerald: Yes, it's only a play, and we were just rehearsing the scripts.

(Mrs. Dooley is too fickle to argue right now, so she abandons the debate. Kellie is still suspicious as to why Barbara and Diamerald are rehearsing a play right now, considering that Mr. Dooley is in such a bad condition, but she also lets it go. Mrs. Dooley invites them to come over and sit with the family in the waiting room. Then Diamerald Alexis calls her best friend, Hanna, to give her the lowdown on her allegedly newfound sibling . . .)

Phone: Hello? Capers' residence.

Diamerald: Oh hi, Ms. Capers, how are you? This is D.A. Is Hanna there?

Ms. Capers: Hi sweetie. I'm doing just fine, thank you, and how are you and your family?

Diamerald: (Thinking again about her dad's situation and gets emotional) Well Ms. Capers, to be honest, we are not doing too good.

Ms. Capers: Oh, I'm sorry to hear that, dear. What's wrong?

Diamerald: (Is now crying) It's my dad, Ms. Capers; he's been hurt and is in the hospital, having surgery performed on him right now.

Ms. Capers: Oh my God! Surgery?! What happened to him, baby? I am so sorry to hear this. What hospital is he in? (Hanna walks into the room that her mom is in. She overhears the conversation and gets excited and sad. She then begins to beg her mom for the phone, so Diamerald does not get a chance to tell Ms. Capers what happened to her dad.)

Ms. Capers: Okay, D.A., thanks for letting us know. We will be praying for your dad, and we will be up there to see you all as soon as I can find something to put on, alright dear? . . . Here's Hanna; she's been trying to pull the phone out of my hands ever since she realized it was you.

Hanna: Hey, girl friend. What's going on with your dad?

Diamerald: He's been hurt by those guys we were hiding from.

Hanna: Really girl?! I'm glad he sent those officers to get us from school then, because if they did that to your dad, who's a cop, there's no telling what they might've done to you and I.

Diamerald: Yeah, I know. By the way, Hanna, did you ever tell your mom about any of that stuff?

Hanna: Girl, I wouldn't dare tell momma! You know how excited she can get; she probably would've had a heart attack. Then I might have wound up as an orphan or something.

Diamerald: Hanna, you're crazy girl.

Hanna: Yeah, I know, but you know I'm being honest about how my momma is.

Diamerald: Uh-huh, but enough small talk. Are you getting ready to come up here with your momma? Because I got something to tell you, girl.

Hanna: What?! What is it?! Now, you know how I am when it comes to gossip.

Diamerald: Yes, I do; that's exactly why I'm waiting to tell you in person, so you won't go running your mouth to your mom.

Hanna: My mom?! What could you say that I would want momma to know?

Diamerald: It makes you wonder, doesn't it?

Hanna: (now eager more than ever to get off the phone) Alright, I gotta go.

Diamerald: Where are you going, Hanna?

Hanna: I'm fixing to go in here and hurry momma, so we can get on up there to the hospital and see about your dad.

Diamerald: Yeah right! Okay, silly girl, I'll see you all soon. Bye.

Hanna: Bye, sister.

(Hearing Hanna call her "sister" reminds Diamerald of the situation at hand, so she gets a bit emotional again. She starts to say something to Hanna about it but decides not to, and just hangs up instead.

Meanwhile, a couple of lawyers have called Major Stephens {who is still at the hospital} from her office back at the police station. They told her that they were there in representation of the four boys that are being detained for further questioning. They've also threatened that if the boys weren't released immediately, they would charge Major Stephens and the other arresting officers with a crime. Chief McClemens has also called Major Stepehens from the D.A.'s office, and instructed her to release the boys ASAP, so in obedience to her superiors, she told an officer to release all four boys immediately, overlooking Agent Archie's order, which was to hold the boys until he said differently . . . All of the boys' parents have gone to pick them up, along with Little Jimmy's grandma, Ms. Nuttingham . . . Little Jimmy is now in the car with Ms. Nuttingham. Before cranking the car, Ms. Nuttingham decides to ask him what happened . . .)

Ms. Nuttingham: June Bug, wut did you and dose uda litta fellas do fa da polices to locks ya'll up?

Little Jimmy: (lying) Nothin', granny, we wasn't doing nothin'. If Lieutenant Dooley hadn't interfered, we would not have gone to jail; but that's okay, it's over now and he gotten just what he deserved.

Ms. Nuttingham: Boy, I nose dat you lyin' thru yo teeth. I'ze a mite be ole, but I'ze ain'ts no fool. Dem polices didn't juss get up out theys bed dis monen, and decide to rest dem some chullens. And whys you tawkn bout dat dare Nutenant Doosey like dat? He wuz tryna look out fa you, on-na-count of me.

Little Jimmy: Well, he won't be looking out for nobody else for a while, maybe not ever again.

Ms. Nuttingham: Why ya says dat, June Bug?

Little Jimmy: Because he's probably dead by now.

Ms. Nuttingham: Wut?! You means tu tells me dat you and dem fools down at dat pool hall duns killed a police offasa, June Bug?

Little Jimmy: No, not me granny; Money Mike and Black are the ones who put the whooping on him. And boy did they whoop him! I bet he wa . . . (looks over at Ms. Nuttingham, who is now holding her chest and breathing heavily) You okay, granny? Talk to me, granny! What's wrong?!

(Ms. Nuttingham has blanked out and isn't responding, so Little Jimmy opens the car door, jumps out and starts yelling . . .)

Little Jimmy: Help! Help! Please, somebody help me! My granny is sick! Please, help me!

(Fortunately, there is an officer on her way into the building, who hears him and comes running to his aid . . .)

Officer: What's wrong?

Little Jimmy: My granny is sick and she needs help.

(The officer calls for an ambulance and checks Ms. Nuttingham's pulse. Realizing that it has stopped beating, the officer futilely tries to resuscitate her . . . The ambulance arrives. The E.M.T's load Ms. Nuttingham into the ambulance and rush her to the hospital, working frantically to revive her. The officer drives behind the ambulance, with Little Jimmy in the passenger seat . . . {Her name is Officer Maria Consquella.} . . . She and Little Jimmy have made it to the hospital and are now sitting in the waiting room. {Ironically, they are at the same hospital that Mr. Dooley is at.} Little Jay has just noticed Little Jimmy sitting with the policewoman, and is going over to speak to him . . .)

Little Jay: Hey there, Little Jimmy! What are you doing up here?

Little Jimmy: (diverted by seeing Little Jay, for obvious reasons) Oh, hi there, Little Jay. I'm here with this officer. She brought me here to see about my granny; she's sick.

Little Jay: (not aware that Little Jimmy already knows about his dad) Oh, I'm sorry to hear that. Is she going to be okay?

Little Jimmy: (doesn't want Little Jay to know that he was there when Money Mike and the others assaulted his dad) I'm not sure, but I certainly hope so; she's all I got left, man.

(Little Jimmy starts to cry, and Officer Consquella trys to console him . . .)

Offc. Consquella: There, there, Jimmy. It's going to be okay; don't cry.

Little Jay: Yeah, Little Jimmy, it's going to be alright. God is in charge, and He will make everything okay; just you wait and see. He did it for my dog, Alofus, He's gonna do it for my dad and He can do it for your granny, 'cause ain't nothing too hard for Him.

Little Jimmy: (is now stunned because he knew about the dog but he thought that it was dead, as did he Little Jay's dad) What about Alofus and your dad, Little Jay?

Little Jay: Well, my dog, Alofus, was beaten by some bad men and was left for dead, but God saved his life and gave him another chance to live. Some bad men beat up my dad and left him for dead as well, which is why we're here at the hospital today, but I know that my dad is going to make it out of the woods, because he's a lot smarter than Alofus.

(Little Jimmy is somewhat baffled by Little Jay's allusion to his dad making it out of the woods. For Little Jay is referring to the illustration he was given about Alofus at the M.A.V.A.S.H.)

Little Jimmy: So are you telling me that your dog, Alofus, and your dad are still alive? Boy, are you people lucky!

Little Jay: Yes, they are both still alive; thanks be to God, but Alofus is doing much better than my dad right now. And you said that our family is lucky? Well, we don't believe in luck, because we have faith that God is a healer and it only works if you believe in him Little Jimmy.

(As Little Jay finishes his sentence, a doctor walks out to speak to the Nuttingham family . . .)

Doctor: (talking to Officer Consquella) Hello, ma'am, I am Dr. Wu. Are you a relative of Ms. Nuttingham?

Offc. Consquella: No sir, but this youngster here (pointing to Little Jimmy) is her grandson. He was with her when she took ill.

Dr. Wu: (focuses his attention on Little Jimmy and reaches to shake his hand) Hey there, young man, how are you? I am Dr. Wu. Have you contacted your parents about your grandmother?

Little Jimmy: (rejects the doctor's hand) My parents?! I have no parents, doc. My momma is dead and my dad is in jail for killing her. Granny is the only one I got to look out for me, so if you want to know anything else, you gotta talk to her when she gets better.

(Dr. Wu is sympathetic after hearing that Little Jimmy is alone. For he has some very bad news to disclose . . .)

Dr. Wu: Come here and sit down. (puts his arm around Little Jimmy's shoulder) Son, your granny didn't make it.

(As he looks on with Officer Consquella, Little Jay begins to shed tears. He walks over to Little Jimmy.)

Little Jimmy: What do you mean, she didn't make it? (He thinks that the doctor is referring to his granny not making it to the hospital.) I know my granny is here 'cause I saw them roll her in here, so why are you lying to me, man? (Now yelling) Where is she?! Where did ya'll put my granny?!

Offc. Consquella: (attempting to calm Little Jimmy) Hey, Little Jimmy, settle down. That's not what he meant. Please, settle down, son; I have something to tell you.

(Little Jimmy quiets down and looks into Officer Consquella's eyes as she speaks.)

Offc. Consquella: Son what the doctor means is that your granny is dead, baby.

Little Jimmy: Dead?! No, granny ain't dead! She can't be dead; I need my granny No!

(Little Jimmy begins to run down the hall, and going from room to room, yelling "Granny! Where are you granny?!" Officer Consquella and the doctor encompasses him and subdues him. Then the doctor orders a nurse to sedate him to calm him down. Little Jay is still looking on and is also very hurt, so he runs to tell Mark and the rest of his family the bad news . . . He arrives back at the kid's waiting room. He begins to tell Mark about Little Jimmy being at the hospital and why he was there. The rest of the family comes in to check on him and Mark and to inform them of Mr. Dooley's condition. Sergeant Willansby, Major Stephens, and Barbara joins them . . .)

Little Jay: (with mixed feelings of sorrow, animation, and anticipation) Guess what, everybody . . . Little Jimmy is up here at the hospital!

Mrs. Dooley: Okay, Little Jay, we hear. ("So does everyone else", Diamerald proclaims.) Now just settle down and tell us what you want us to know.

(After hearing Little Jimmy's name being mentioned, Sergeant Willansby and Major Stephens are also interested in what Little Jay has to say now.)

Little Jay: As I was saying, mom, Little Jimmy is here in the hospital right now. I just finished talking to him (pointing) right down there.

Mrs. Dooley: Why is Little Jimmy here at the hospital?

Serg. Willansby and Maj. Stephens: (Simultaneously) Yeah, why is he?

Little Jay: (beckons for everyone to follow him) Come on, he's down here; I'll show you all.

(Everyone walks down the hall to where Little Jimmy and Officer Consquella were last seen. Upon arrival, Major Stephens and Sergeant Willansby recognize their fellow officer, and vice versa . . .)

Offc. Consquella: (shakes Major Stephens' and Sergeant Willansby's hands) Hello there, Major Stephens, and Sergeant Willansby. So what brings you all here?

Maj. Stephens: That was going to be my question to you, Officer Consquella. Anyhow, we are here on official business. Now what's your reason for being here, might I ask?

Offc. Consquella: Well, ma'am, you wouldn't believe it but after leaving the department, I was walking to my vehicle, getting ready to head home when all of a sudden, I heard this kid yelling for help. I turned to pinpoint his whereabouts and ran to his aid. Once there, I noticed that there was an elderly woman slumped over in the vehicle. She was non-responsive. The kid said that she was his grandmother, and that his name was Little Jimmy. Anyhow, I tried to resuscitate her but to no avail, so I called 911 . . . and here we are.

Serg. Willansby: Did you say that Little Jimmy's grandmother was sick, and is now here in the hospital?

Offc. Consquella: Yeah, but she is no longer sick, Sergeant Willansby; unfortunately, she didn't make it.

Maj. Stephens: Oh my God! No! What happened to her?

Offc. Consquella: Well, the doctor said that she had a vast myocardial infarction.

Maj. Stephens: What on earth is that?

Serg. Willansby: That's just some fancy name for a massive heart attack; I remember them using those same words when my mom passed away.

Offc. Consquella: Poor kid . . . My understanding is that she was all he had left.

Serg. Willansby: Yes, that's what Lieutenant Dooley told me.

Maj. Stephens: Lieutenant Dooley?! What does he have to do with this?

Serg. Willansby: Well, you see, Lieut. Doo . . . (Mrs. Dooley interrupts.)

Mrs. Dooley: Major Stephens, my husband was first acquainted with those two individuals after a controversy arose between our boy, Little Jay here and Little Jimmy. He went over to converse with Little Jimmy's grandmother, Ms. Melba Nuttingham. She and Jonathan got to know each other briefly and he vowed to help her get Little Jimmy off the streets. He seemed to be fully committed in keeping his word, too. It's so unfortunate for her to have left before she could see this come to fruition. I'm sure if Jonathan wasn't already half dead, this would kill him. For he seemed to have taken a great liking to Ms. Nuttingham. He said that she sort of reminded him of his late mom. Anyhow, where is Little Jimmy? I haven't seen him since Jonathan spoke to his grandmother. Before then, he used to come over our house regularly to play with Little Jay.

Offc. Consquella: Oh, he's down there in room 221. The doctor had a nurse to sedate him after he heard about his grandmother's passing because he got very irate.

Diamerald: You know what, ya'll? Some of us don't know how blessed we are until we hear these kinds of stories.

Kellie: Yeah, baby, you are so right, but God knows what He is doing; let's not forget that.

Shawn: Of course He does, Kellie, but we, still being in human form, can't always grasp the significance surrounding His actions. I guess that's why He tells us His ways are not our ways and His thoughts are not our thoughts.

Serg. Willansby: You got that right, Mr. Hogan.

Barbara: Yeah. Listening to all that has gone on with Uncle Dooley, Ms. Nuttingham, and mom's recent abduction helps us to count our blessings, because even when we think that we have lost everything, God shows us that we have so much more to be thankful for.

Kellie: Amen to that, young lady, and I hope and pray that we all take notes on this learning experience.

Little Jay: Mom, can Mark and I go down to see Little Jimmy?

Mrs. Dooley: I don't see why not, as long as the doctor says it's okay, honey.

(Hanna and Ms. Capers are walking toward Diamerald and her family. Diamerald greets them with a hug.)

Diamerald: Hey Hanna; hi Ms. Capers; 'glad you all made it safely.

Ms. Capers: Yeah, and so am I. For a moment, I thought we would be brought in by an ambulance.

Diamerald: Why'd you say that, Ms. Capers?

Ms. Capers: Because your friend here, "Ms. Fast Feet", was driving like a bat out of hell. I started not to let her drive, but she insisted, because she claimed that I drive like an old lady.

Hanna: Momma, please, now you know that it wasn't as bad as you're saying. I drove the speed limit, didn't I?

Ms. Capers: Yeah, the speed limit for the highway, but we also drove down a couple of streets to get here, or did you forget?

(Mrs. Dooley interrupts their reciprocating conversation.)

Mrs. Dooley: Hey there, Kim, how have things been going for you?

Ms. (Kim) Capers: Things are going just fine, Lillian. I know you cut me and Hanna off on purpose; but the real question is, how you doing? I am so sorry to hear about Jonathan's unfortunate situation.

Mrs. Dooley: Yeah, me too, girl. It's been a nightmare; all that this family has been going through, and it ain't over.

Ms. Capers: I know what you mean, but just keep holding on to God's steady hands.

(The two of them walk off to continue their conversation in private, and Hanna and Diamerald do the same . . .)

Hanna: (talking to Diamerald) Okay, now what did you have to tell me?

Diamerald: See there, girl; I knew it. I thought you were in such a hurry to get up here to see about my dad. You haven't asked me one thing about him since you got here.

Hanna: Oh, my bad. How is he doing, really?

Diamerald: Yeah, you sound very concerned (being sarcastic). Anyway, he isn't so well. They beat him up pretty badly, and he will need several operations to return to normal, if that's possible.

Hanna: Girl, you know what they taught us in Sunday school; with God, anything is possible, so just keep the faith, D.A . . . Now, what did you want to tell me?

Diamerald: That was quick and to the point, Hanna. I sure am glad to have a friend as caring as you.

Hanna: So what're you saying, D. A.; that I'm being inconsiderate or something?

Diamerald: No, Hanna, I wouldn't dare call you out like that; it's just that your timing is off, that's all. But before I give you the scoop, I have a question for you, okay?

Hanna: Alright, let's have it.

Diamerald: (puts her finger on her chin, as in deep thought) Let's see now . . . Okay, Hanna, how would you feel if you found out that you had an older sister?

Hanna: What?! You got a sister, D. A.?!

Diamerald: A question usually beggets an answer, not another question, Hanna. Now would you mind answering me before you pose your own question?

Hanna: Well, to be honest, it depends on two things.

Diamerald: Really? And now what might those two things be silly girl?

Hanna: First of all, would she be wealthy? And secondly, would she be prettier than me?

Diamerald: Girl, I'm serious.

Hanna: So am I, D.A.

Diamerald: Okay, then what if she was prettier than you and poor, Hanna?

Hanna: Then I wouldn't claim her because she'd have nothing to offer me but trouble with my potential boyfriends, and it wouldn't be worth it.

Diamerald: You know what, Hanna? I believe you are serious, girl.

Hanna: Does it look like I'm kidding here? (Then she starts to laugh.) But seriously, D. A., I would be thrilled. As a matter of fact, that's why you and I are so close, because I've always wanted an older sister or brother but my mom said she couldn't have any more children due to something about her health.

Diamerald: Okay Hanna, I believe you now girl, but I was really kind of hoping you wouldn't be down with it.

Hanna: Why?

Diamerald: Because I think I do have an older sister, and even though I'm not one hundred percent certain, I'm not happy about it.

Hanna: What makes you think such a thing, D.A.?

Diamerald: Well, I overheard Sergeant Willansby talking to her daughter, Barbara, and Barbara asked Sergeant Willansby if she forgot that someone was her dad. She was referring to my dad, Hanna, I just know it!

Hanna: Are you sure about what you heard, D.A.? I mean, couldn't she have been talking about someone else?

Diamerald: As I said, Hanna, I'm not one hundred percent sure, but I am ninety-nine.

Hanna: (being sarcastic) Well, the law says that you have to be ninety-nine point nine percent sure to be legit . . . Anyhow girl, I know you didn't tell your momma any of this, did you?

Diamerald: No way! I don't wanna upset my mom any more than she already is. I'm just gonna leave it alone until dad gets better . . . if he gets better. Then I'll ask him about it.

Hanna: (trying to reassure Diamerald about her dad's recovery) Now D.A., you know that your dad is a fighter. Not only is he going to get better; he's gonna come back even greater than he was before, just wait and see. And one more thing, D.A.: what's so bad about Barbara being your sister? I think she's cool and cute.

Diamerald: So do I, and I'm not worried about her taking any of my potential boyfriends either. I guess everything that has recently transpired has gotten me thinking irrationally or something, but I guess it will all work itself out in the end; perhaps for the good.

Hanna: Yeah, it will. Now I'm hungry; where's the snack shop around here?

(They both walk down the hall to find a snack shop. Meanwhile, Little Jay and Mark have made it to Little Jimmy's room. Little Jay is about to speak to him . . .)

Little Jay: Hello there, Little Jimmy. How are you feeling?

Little Jimmy: Oh, I'm alright, but the doctor seemed to think I lost it because I got all crazy after he told me that my granny was dead. What would he or anyone else have done if it was their grandma?

Little Jay: Yeah, I understand how you feel, Little Jimmy, because I cried when I lost my granny. As a matter of fact, both of my grannies are gone. My mom's mom passed away a little over a year ago. She, my granddad, and their dog were all killed in a car wreck on their way home.

Little Jimmy: Yeah, but you still got your mom and dad; I don't have anybody left to help me.

Mark: I may not know you very well, Little Jimmy, but I can tell you this much: in our Sunday school class, we learned that when ones mom and dad forsakes them, God would be there to take them up. That's found in the 27th chapter and 10th verse of the book of Psalms. Also, in the 49th chapter of Isaiah, verses 15 through 16, God said that a woman might forget her child, but He won't forget His children.

Little Jay: So Little Jimmy, the lesson here is that if we belong to Him, He will see us through til the end.

Little Jimmy: Man, I never took you to be the religious type, Little Jay. And your cousin, Mark, really seems to know that Bible stuff. Boy, you guys must really listen in the Sunday school class! I mean, I went on occasions, but only because my granny made me. I thought I'd never need any of that stuff, but I guess I was wrong, huh?

Mark: Of course you were if you thought that you wouldn't ever need God, Little Jimmy.

Little Jimmy: I didn't say that I didn't need God; I said that Bible stuff.

Mark: Well, that Bible stuff is God, Little Jimmy. In the first chapter of St. John, first and fourteenth verses, it tells us that the Word is God. The Word was in the very beginning, and it came down to us in the flesh. We beheld it as the only begotten of the Father, Jesus Christ, our Savior.

Little Jimmy: So if the bible is God, then when we read it, God is talking to us, right?

Little Jay: You got it! Boy, you're pretty smart too, Little Jimmy, and you catch on fast! I'm sure that God could use a guy like you.

Little Jimmy: You really think that he would want someone like me, Little Jay? . . . I don't know; I've been pretty bad lately.

Mark: It doesn't matter how bad you've been, Little Jimmy. As long as you're ready to stop being bad, God is ready and willing to help you clean up your life.

Little Jimmy: Okay, then I'm ready. What do I have to do for him to help me?

Mark: You don't have to do anything. Just believe in your heart and confess it with your mouth and you shall be saved.

Little Jimmy: Saved?! What does that mean?

Little Jay: That just means that you've been accepted as one of His dear children, and that He will never leave you nor forsake you. He will always be with you, even until the end of the world.

Little Jimmy: Boy, that sounds awesome! Who wouldn't want to be a part of that?

Mark: You'd be amazed, Little Jimmy; there are a lot of people who choose not to be a part of all that . . . but as for you, I'm going to ask you to repeat after me, okay?

Little Jimmy: Alright.

Mark: Lord, God of Abraham, Isaac, and Jacob, I, Little Jimmy, come before the throne of grace to tell you that I do believe that you sent your son, Jesus Christ, to die for, not only my sins, but for the sins of the world. I believe that he rose on the third day and went back to glory to sit on that great white throne. I confess it with my mouth and believe it in my heart.

(Little Jimmy repeats every word.)

Little Jimmy: Now what?

Little Jay: Now you're saved, Little Jimmy, and you are one of his sheep; and all the angels in heaven are rejoicing over you.

Little Jimmy: Really?! That's deep!

Mark: No, that's high, Little Jimmy; way up there above the stars, the moon, and beyond.

Little Jay: Actually, Mark, Little Jimmy has a point. The Word of God does get deep, deep into the marrow of the bone.

Little Jimmy: Okay, let's not get so deep that I get lost here.

Mark: No, Little Jimmy, you were lost but are now are found; and you were also blind but now you see, as the scripture declares.

Little Jay: You see, Little Jimmy, the god of this world had blinded you due to your unbelief in the Lord, Jesus Christ, but now the true and living God has opened your eyes to Him, because He is the way, the truth, and the life, and the only way to come to the Father is by Him.

(Just as Little Jay completes this remark, Diamerald Alexus walks in to get him and Mark. For the doctor has asked everyone to meet him in the family room to discuss Mr. Dooley's prognosis. So they all head out down the hall, where the rest of the family is waiting . . .)

(Everyone is now in the family room, waiting for the doctor. He comes in and begins to speak . . .)

Dr. Shaderi: Is the entire Dooley family here?

Mrs. Dooley: Yes, Doctor Shaderi. Now can we please get on with this? The anticipation of the inevitable is killing me.

Dr. Shaderi: Okay, Mrs. Dooley, I understand. Well, to get straight to the point, Mr. Dooley's chances of survival are slim to none, and the only hope for him is some sort of miracle.

Kelly: Well, there it is; that's our cue.

Hanna: Oh my God, D.A.; your Aunt Kellie has lost it! What on earth is she talking about?

Diamerald: No, Hanna, my aunt ain't crazy; she just got Jesus. You know how the commercial says, "Got milk"? . . . Well, she got Jesus.

Dr. Shaderi: (Being sarcastic) Well alright then, we desparately could use that man on our side.

Kelly: Hold on, Doc . . . First of all, He ain't no man, nor is He the son of a man that He should lie.

(Dr. Shaderi looks at everyone and replies . . .)

Dr. Shaderi: Ooo . . . kay; whatever that means.

Mrs. Dooley: What that means, Doctor Shaderi, is that the God we serve is not like you and I. Therefore, He is not limited to healing, but is able to do above and beyond all that we ask of Him, because nothing is too hard or impossible for Him.

Kellie: Hallelujah and amen to that, sister.

Mrs. Dooley: Now on that note, what exactly are you supposing to do, Dr. Shaderi?

Dr. Shaderi: After hearing such faith based testimonies, the only thing to do here is open the floor for suggestions, ma'am.

Diamerald: Well, I think that we ought to call Professor Greer and Dr. Kyzar in on this discussion.

Dr. Shaderi: If you don't mind my asking younglady, who are they?

Mrs. Dooley: They're the doctors who assisted in our dog, Alofus' surgery.

Dr. Shaderi: Please excuse my candor, but I'm lost here. What exactly could a veterinarian do for Mr. Dooley, dear?

Diamerald: Yeah, you are lost, Doc, because they're not just veterinarians; they're Doctors of biophysis bionics and prosthetists for both man and beast.

Dr. Shaderi: (being sarcastic) Now that was very helpful . . . And I got it; So you want us to make your dad like Steve Austin, the character portrayed in "The Six Million Dollar Man", television show, right?

(Everyone looks at Dr. Shaderi, as if to say, "Well yeah, why not?" and Diamerald goes out on a limb and asks . . .)

Diamerald: And why not, Dr. Shaderi?

Dr. Shaderi: Why? I'll tell you why. For one, it would be very expensive, if at all possible. And secondly, I don't think that the law would allow for such a ridiculous thing.

Kellie: Again, Dr. Shaderi, with God nothing is impossible; and money is no object where He is concerned. For all the gold and silver is His, and He has cattle on a thousand hills.

Dr. Shaderi: Then let's hope that He's willing to release some of that gold and start selling some of those cattle, because it's going to cost a lot of milk, butter, and money to accomplish what you all are suggesting here, honey.

Sergt. Willansby: To be in the healthcare business, you are a rather pessimistic character, Dr. Shaderi when it comes to healing.

Kellie: It doesn't matter about his unbelief, Sergeant Willansby, because if it's God's will for my brother-in-law, Jonathan, to recover from this ordeal, nothing will hinder the forwarding effort, not even economics.

Dr. Shaderi: No, people, I'm not a pessimist, but I am a realist, someone you all might consider becoming, so that you can see the reality of the situation here.

Diamerald: Dr. Shaderi, isn't it somewhere in you all's medical creed of law, that states, doctors should have faith in something other than themselves? Afterall, wasn't Jesus the epitome of healing? I know one thing for sure, I wouldn't want any of you doubting Thomas' operating on me.

Dr. Shaderi: Okay enough of this, I'm not going to get into a debate with you all over your religious beliefs. However, when all is said and done, we will have to run this matter by our chief physician here at St. Mary's, Dr. Sheila Zanettoe. So if you all will excuse me, I will head on up to her office right now; we don't have a lot of time here. (Everyone agrees that time is of the essence, so they stop talking and allow Dr. Shaderi to go speak with Dr. Zanettoe about Mr. Dooley's situation. As everyone heads back to the waiting area, Mrs. Dooley gets a call from the M.A.V.A.S.H., the veterinarian hospital where Alofus is being held . . .)

Phone: Hello, is this Mrs. Dooley?

Mrs. Dooley: Yes, this is she, and who am I speaking with?

Phone: This is Dr. Smortzen, head of surgery operations over at the M.A.V.A.S.H.

Mrs. Dooley: Oh yeah, now I remember. Please excuse me for not recognizing your voice, Dr. Smortzen. You see, our lives have taken a rather drastic change since we last talked.

Dr. Smortzen: Well, I am sorry to hear that, Mrs. Dooley, but I was calling to give you some good news about Alofus.

Mrs. Dooley: Really?! What is it, Dr. Smortzen?

Dr. Smortzen: Oh, it's nothing, except that Alofus is up and about, barking, and responding to various commands at an abnormal rate.

Mrs. Dooley: Oh my God! Are you serious, Dr. Smortzen?! Is he really doing all those things?!

(Mrs. Dooley's excitement has gotten Kellie and Diamerald's attention.)

Diamerald: (talking to Mrs. Dooley) Who are you talking to, mom? What are you talking about?

(Mrs. Dooley is now about to tell everyone the good news. She asks Dr. Smortzen if he could hold on a minute while she does so . . .)

Mrs. Dooley: Honey, that was Dr. Smortzen from over at the M.A.V.A.S.H. He was calling to inform us of the changes in Alofus's condition.

Diamerald: Really? I hope it's some good news, because I can use some of that right about now.

Kellie: Yeah, we all can Diamerald. So what did Dr. Smortzen say about the miracle dog, Lillian?

Mrs. Dooley: He said that Alofus was up, running around and barking.

Dr. Smortzen: I don't mean to interrupt you, but I do have to get back to work on something. However you all are more than welcome to come in and further discuss Alofus' progress with Professor Greer and Dr. Kyzar; you can even see it first hand.

Mrs. Dooley: Oh, okay then, Dr. Smortzen; we will do just that. I'm going to find Little Jay and we will be right over.

Dr. Smortzen: Great; I know he will be thrilled to hear the good news. I'll see you all shortly . . . goodbye.

(Mrs. Dooley turns to tell everyone that they are about to head back to the M.A.V.A.S.H. Then she asks Diamerald and Hanna to get Little Jay and Mark. As they do, she walks over to the receptionist and lets her know that they are about to leave the hospital for a while. She also asks her to let Dr. Shaderi know that they will return to hear what the chief physician had to say about Mr. Dooley. Then Mrs. Dooley asks the protective officers to escort her and the family back to the M.A.V.A.S.H . . .)

(About twenty minutes later, the entire crew arrives back at the M.A.V.A.S.H along with the officers. Everyone heads inside. Mrs. Dooley goes and speaks with the receptionist, who tells her that Dr. Smortzen was expecting them and points them in the direction to meet up with him . . . They have reached Dr. Smortzen and he is now greeting them . . .)

Dr. Smortzen: Well, hello there, people; nice to see you all again.

(Dr. Smortzen beckons for everyone to follow him into the corridor, where Alofus is being housed.)

(Upon entering the door, Little Jay immediately notices Alofus and he and Mark start running toward him, but they are abruptly intervened and haulted by security. Dr. Smortzen is about to address the situation . . .)

Dr. Smortzen: Please excuse our security patrol, Little Jay and Mark, but they have been ordered to keep any and everyone away from your dog, Alofus. For he is now top secret, and is also partially owned by the federal government and a personal investor, who insists on remaining nameless in this project.

Mrs. Dooley: Top secrect?! Owned by the federal government?! What on earth are you talking about, Dr. Smortzen?

Diamerald: (now very irate) Yeah, Alofus belongs to us, not the federal government or anybody else! And what's all this "top secret" stuff?

(Little Jay, Kellie, and everyone else collectively murmurs about Dr. Smortzen's bold and surprising statement. Professor Greer and Dr. Kyzar walk in on all the commotion . . .)

Dr. Smortzen: (yelling to get everyone's attention) People, please . . . settle down here, and I will try and do my best to explain, okay? . . . (Everyone quiets down) . . . Now everyone is obviously upset over my precipitance, and I must admit, I should have taken a more deliberate approach on informing you all of the situation at hand; although, Mrs. Dooley, I did think that you and your husband understood that, by signing the paper work, you authorized me as the supervisor for Alofus' operation. Nonetheless, I'm sorry to have to tell you all such unexpectedly bad news. However, this does not excuse the reality of the matter here, which is that one-third of your dog, Alofus, is now legally owned by the federal government and one third is legally owned by the anonymous investor. As rude and presumptious as it may sound, had not it been for these other participants, Alofus would not even be here for us to debate this issue at all. So I don't mean to sound callous or obstinate, I just thought that I should disclose certain information, especially something as grave as this.

(After listening to Dr. Smortzen explain the stipulations of Alofus' ownership, Professor Greer decides to interject a few words of her own, hoping to give the Dooleys a more thourough understanding of what Dr. Smortzen has just said . . .)

Prof. Greer: (smiling while looking at Mrs. Dooley and her family, trying to mollify the mood) Well, hello there, lovely people; it's good to see you all again. How is everybody doing?

Diamerald: Not too good, Professor Greer, as I'm sure you can see. Maybe you can shed a little light on this bomb that your pal, Dr. Smortzen here, has just dropped on our hearts.

Prof. Greer: Well, Diamerald, Alofus is still you all's dog, but being a new, top-secret innovation, he is now somewhat of a lethal weapon and must be registered with the federal government because if he was to be duplicated and used maliciously, he would be a great threat to society. As for the individual who helped fund the operation, he just wants to keep an eye on his investment.

Mrs. Dooley: Investment?! Did you just call our dog an investment, as if he is some sort of commodity, Professor Greer? Where do you all get off, concluding such a ridiculous notion?

(Seeing how upset all of this is making Mrs. Dooley, in addition to the emotional stress that she has undergone while trying to cope with Mr. Dooley's recent hospitalization, Kellie walks over to her sister and tries to comfort her . . .)

Kellie: (while hugging Mrs. Dooley) Okay Lillian, settle down, sweetie. I know how upsetting it must be to hear such scandalous rhetoric, but you must understand, first and foremost, sis, that we all prayed and gave this thing to the Lord. And with that being said . . . well, as I'm sure you already know, all things work together for the good of them that love Him, Lillian; and I know that we love Him, so let's take a back seat and let him work his miracle, to see what the end shall be, alright honey?

Mrs. Dooley: (turns and looks directly into Kellie's eyes) You know, I thank God for giving me such a great sister, and thank you for caring enough to shake my coat tail, so to speak, when needed. You are absolutely right on this, and now I know why the bible tells us that two are better than one. I'm glad that you are the one who supports me at times like these, reminding me that God should be the focal point in my life and decision making . . . (Turns to Dr. Smortzen) . . . Now back to you, Dr. Smortzen, Professor Greer, and

Dr. Kyzar: will you all please excuse my family and I for our outburst and senseless reaction to what you told us about Alofus?

Dr. Smortzen: No apoplogy is necessary, Mrs. Dooley. For we all understand how you feel, and you and your family's actions were completely justified. Besides, had it been either of us, I'm sure we all would've reacted the very same way, so please don't go beating yourself up, okay dear? . . . And here's another piece that I forgot to add to the puzzle of Alofus' subservience: It was agreed that the others will have ownership for a limited amount of time; afterward, you will regain absolute jurisdiction as Alofus' rightful owners.

Diamerald: Limited time, huh Doc? And just what does that mean? That our dog was lent out or something?

Dr. Smortzen: Well, as strange as that might sound, yes, he was, young lady . . . In lame-man's terms, that's precisely what it means. You see, the federal government wants us to ensure the reliability of allowing Alofus to be in the company of humans without the strict need of security. As for the investor . . . well, as Professor Greer stated earlier, he just wants to be assured that he will be the first one notified on the progress and success of his investment, but more importantly, that he will reap the dividends due him, be it political or monitary, if you get where I'm coming from, people.

Mrs. Dooley: Yes, unfortunately, Dr. Smortzen, we do get where you are coming from, and where this is going as well, but I'm not going to get into that. As my sister, Kellie said, it's all in God's hands now. So can Little Jay, Mark, and Diamerald at least go over and give Alofus a rub, and perhaps take a couple of pictures with him?

Dr. Smortzen: Unfortunately, Mrs. Dooley, no photos are allowed at this point and time, and hopefully, within a couple of days or so, we will be able to determine the feasibility of a possible rub session. However you all are permitted to see the progression in some of Alofus' activities, such as running and barking, but that's all that we can allow for now.

Mrs. Dooley: Well, if that's all we get, then that's all we get. Let's see the dog bark, Dr. Smortzen.

(Dr. Smortzen calls for the guy who has been attending to Alofus and asks him to demonstrate some of the activities that they have accomplished thus far, so in comes the guy to show off Alofus' skills . . .)

Guy: (walks over to Alofus) S-K9, heel! . . . Heel, S-K9!

(Alofus raises his left leg and paw and points them back toward the floor, directly beside himself. Then he immediately jumps to his feet, runs over to the guy, and squats down on his rump. Everyone in the Dooley group starts to murmur amongst themselves; all but Diamerald, who openly speaks out . . .)

Diamerald: What the !!##$@? . . .

(Diamerald doesn't complete her sentence, yet Little Jay, Mark, and Hanna all interject . . .)

Little Jay, Mark, and Hanna: (simultaneously) Ooh . . .

Mrs. Dooley: Diamerald, I know you didn't just use profanity in my presence!

Kellie: No, I know she didn't just use it period, Lillian.

Diamerald: No ma'am, I didn't, but I almost. Did anybody else here, hear what that guy just called Alofus, or was it just me?

Mrs. Dooley: Yeah, I heard him, too, honey, but I thought that he was just using some special code word or something. Please enlighten us, Dr. Smortzen. Don't tell us that the guy was calling our dog by name.

Dr. Smortzen: Well, to be frank, people, he was calling the dog by that name. However, like the ownership stipulation, the name is also temporary, okay?

Diamerald: No, Doc, it's not okay! (Turns to Little Jay) Little Jay, speak up; don't be afraid. Let them know how you feel about them calling your dog "S-K9"; whatever the heck that means.

Little Jay: Well, to be honest, Dr. Smortzen, I really don't like you guys calling Alofus another name. For the name he has is very special and dear to all of us. You see, God gave me that name in a dream, and I don't want him getting mad at us for changing it. Why would you do such a thing without talking it over with me first anyway, Dr. Smortzen?

Mrs. Dooley: Son, as I always say, you are exceptionally special. The way you conveyed your feelings to Dr. Smortzen was very articulate . . . So go ahead now, Dr. Smortzen, explain your way out of this one.

Dr. Smortzen: Okay, gladly . . . if everyone would just hold their tongues for a few minutes while I explain. Now as I was saying before being interrupted, people, the name is not permanent. It was only assigned to your dog to signify the phase in which we carried out the operation, and to underscore the secrecy of the innovation at hand. You see, S-K9 is merely an abbreviation for Stealth Canine. We, in conjunction with the federal government, decided to give Alofus this name; and what better way to describe Alofus' skillful and clever craftiness and, at the same time, achieve the very purpose of a specific goal, being that some of his body parts are artificial and specifically designed to go undetected? . . . So there you have it folks; that's how the name came about. By no means did we ever intend to disserve or disrespect you, Little Jay, or your family. And if you all just give us a few more weeks, we will allow you to come over to participate in the therapeutic membrane sessions. However, those sessions will not be held here; they will be at the Mount Woodville facility in West, Virgina for precautionary reasons, as I stated earlier; so be prepared to travel, people. I hope that I have answered you all's question in regards to this matter, and that you all will forgive me for not doing so sooner.

Mrs. Dooley: You most certainly have, Dr. Smortzen, and yes, we do forgive you; I'm sure that I'm speaking on behalf of everyone in the room. After hearing your explanation . . . well, it just makes sense, and we don't want to get in the way any longer, or hinder the ongoing success of Alofus' recovery. I, or should I say we, would like to thank you and everyone involved for the care and nurture that has been given to Alofus thus far; we greatly appreciate everything.

Dr. Smortzen: And thank you for your candor and support, Mrs. Dooley. I'm sure that I too speak on behalf of everyone that has anything to do with Alofus' care; and we accept and appreciate you all's compliments.

Mrs. Dooley: And on that note, Dr. Smortzen, Professor Greer, and Dr. Kyzar, I am sorry to say that we are going to have to depart. For we have some more pressing and important business to attend to back at Saint Mary's Hospital.

Prof. Greer: Saint Mary's?! Really, Mrs. Dooley?! I mean, please excuse my rather blunt line of questioning here, but I'm just curious as to what could be more important than your dog Alofus right now.

Mrs. Dooley: Well, it's nice of you to ask, Professr Greer, but I was about to tell you all anyhow . . . It's my husband, Jonathan. You see, he's been hu . . . (Mrs. Dooley is now getting emotional and cannot continue, so Kellie is about to take over with the story behind Mr. Dooley's trauma . . .)

Kellie: You see, folks, what my sister was trying to tell you all is that her husband, Lieutenant Dooley, has been hurt.

Three associates: (talking under their breath) What happened? Is he alright?

Kellie: Actually, no, he isn't. As a matter of fact, his very life is in peril . . .

(Kellie is interrupted by Professor Greer.)

Prof. Greer: In peril?! Oh my God; not Lieutenant Dooley! Let me take a wild guess here; it has something to do with our chief of police and that darn Dr. Elenski, doesn't it?

(Professor Greer's statement gets everyone's attention, especially Mrs. Dooley's, whose composure changes immediately after hearing it . . .)

Mrs. Dooley: Why on earth would you suspect our police chief in my husband's assault, and call out a name that we and others have already deemed as a possible suspect as well? Is there something that you'd like to tell us Prof. Greer? Because I don't believe that it was a mere coincidence for you to make such a bold statement.

(Mrs. Dooley also finds it strange that neither she nor her sister, Kellie, ever finished telling the story about Mr. Dooley's situation, yet Professor Greer had an idea of who was in on it; so this definitely puts a twist on things. Professor Greer is about to address Mrs. Dooley's question . . .)

Prof. Greer: Yes, there is something that I can tell you all, Mrs. Dooley, but I don't know if it will be helpful in apprehending any suspects. Nonetheless, I want you to know that I plan on giving you all my complete solidarity on this matter, until the culprit is apprehended. So what I have to tell you is that our chief of police, Chief McClemens, is working with Dr. Elenski to further some sinister and devious acts.

Mrs. Dooley: And what might those be, Professor Greer, if you don't mind me asking?

Prof. Greer: Well, to get straight to the point, Dr. Elenski has been working on an experiment for quite some time now, trying to recreate the human body as you and I know it, people.

Diamerald: (seclusively speaking to Hanna) Oh boy, here she goes again, girl . . . talking about that crazy stuff that she was trying to get us to believe in class.

Hanna: I don't know, Diamerald; I kinda believe some of that stuff, girl. Even though I'm still trying to figure out the part about a person being dead; now that I don't believe.

Mrs. Dooley: Just what on earth are you talking about, Professor Greer?

Prof. Greer: I'm talking about Dr. Elenski, my former boss and partner in the science lab over at Jackson State University. He has been

working on a project, trying to reinvent the human body as
you and I know it; and if I may interject here, he has had some
success; this I know for a fact. Had not I seen it with my own
eyes I would not have believed it either, people. But the truth
of the matter is, though this guy is very brilliant, yet he is a
danger to society. That's why he was terminated; and shortly
thereafter, an individual comes up dead.

Kellie: Who came up dead?

Prof. Greer: Dr. Satcher, our former president at Jackson State that's
who; and the police has yet to solve the case, the case that
Sergeant Willansby and Lieutenant Dooley were working on, I
might add. It's ironic that Sergeant Willansby came up missing,
and Lieutenant Dooley has been beaten up and left for dead,
which is why I know that this was no coincidence. Besides,
Lieutenant Dooley and I have discussed this matter in some
degree, and I told him to be careful not to piss Dr. Elenski off;
he can be very difficult to deal with when he gets upset.

Mrs. Dooley: Professor Greer, after hearing all that you had to say in
regards to my husband, our chief, and Dr. Elenski . . . well, I'm
inclined to see some validity to the story. Now with that being
said, Professor Greer, would you be willing to come forward
and testify to what you just said in a court of Law?

Prof. Greer: Um . . . I don't know about that, Mrs. Dooley. For we
have come to notice that everyone who gets involved in this
matter winds up hurt, missing, or worse, dead . . . I'd have to
give that some serious thought. However, I'll tell you what I
will do: I'd be willing to offer my knowledge in medical science
to help reconstruct Lieutenant Dooley pro bono.

*(Everyone begins to murmur about Professor Greer's statement, then Dr.
Smortzen blurts out . . .)*

Dr. Smortzen: Hold on a minute here, Professor Greer . . . Just what are you alluding to, talking about reconstructing the human body? I hope it does not conflict with the ethics of medical science.

Prof. Greer: Please excuse my French, Dr. Smortzen, but to hell with ethics, because medical science is being threatened right now and we need a counter to answer for what this mad man has done.

Kellie: And what exactly has this mad man done, Professor Greer?

Prof. Greer: You mean aside from having Dr. Satcher murdered, orchestrating Sergeant Willansby's abduction, and now, beating Lieutenant Dooley to a pulp? Well, let's just say that he has created a monster to carry out his dirty work.

Diamerald: A monster?! Are you serious, Professor Greer? I mean, come on, now you are talking like someone from an Alfred Hitchcock movie. Do you really believe that stuff that you have been telling us?

Mrs. Dooley: What stuff are you talking about, Diamerald, dear?

Diamerald: I'm sorry, mom, but I'm really too embarrassed to even elaborate on it, because I don't want you to think the wrong thing about our teacher here, or that you and dad have wasted your money own furthering my education.

Hanna: (yelling) Yeah, Mrs. Dooley for real though.Now even though our teacher Professor Greer here is somewhat of a nut case at times! Especially when she told us that this Dr. Elenski guy used a dead man's body and brought it back to life just to prove that his theory works. However I myself beleive that there is some validity to parts of her story, and I think that you guys should listen to her just in case. You know what I'm saying here people.

(The mood drastically changes.)

Kellie: Mark and Little Jay, I think you two should leave the room now. This is way over you guys' heads; only grownups need to be in on this type of discussion. Go and wait in the lobby, ok?

Mark: Ah, mom, that's not fair! If that's the case, then why aren't Hanna and Diamerald being asked to leave? They're not grownups either.

Kellie: But I am a grownup, and I told you to leave; now go, and no more back talk, or you will be seeing the back of my hand.

(Mark and Little Jay both exit the room.)

Mrs. Dooley: Now, Professor Greer, about this monster that you claim that Dr. Elenski has created, this Money Mike character, just how do you suppose we go about apprehending him?

Prof. Greer: Like I said, Mrs. Dooley, the only way you can win against those guys is to fight fire with fire.

Kellie: Yeah, I concur; if you live by the sword, then you should die by the sword.

Diamerald: So what are you saying, Aunt Kellie? An eye for an eye and a tooth for a tooth? Doesn't the bible say that vengence is God's?

Mrs. Dooley: Yes, Diamerald, but the word of God also says that anybody who doesn't take care of his household is worse than an infidel; and thanks to those thugs, your dad is not in a position to take care of anything right now. That's why it's encumbant upon me to carry this mission out for him . . . by making those guys pay for hurting someone in our household.

Prof. Greer: While we're discussing the bible, Diamerald, didn't David slay the giant, Goliath, and cut his head off afterward?

Kellie: Now this is getting better and better; for our chief's head would look pretty good sitting on a shelf somewhere. Wouldn't you say, folks? (Everyone starts to laugh.)

Mrs. Dooley: Okay people, enough talk; I need to head back over to the hospital and attend to some unfinished business I have with Dr. Shaderi.

(Everyone says goodbye, and Professor Greer tells Mrs. Dooley that she and Dr. Kyzar will be right over to check on Mr. Dooley, as soon as they finish their duties at the M.A.V.A.S.H. So Mrs. Dooley and the rest of the crew head back over to St. Mary's hospital . . .)

(They arrive at their destination within mintues. Mrs. Dooley is now at the desk, speaking to the receptionist about Dr. Shaderi.)

Mrs. Dooley: Hello, ma'am, I'm Mrs. Dooley and I was wondering if, by chance, Dr. Shaderi left a message for me.

Recept: Oh yeah, he most certainly did, Mrs. Dooley. You all are to go up to speak with Dr. Zanettoe; she's on the fourth floor of the south wing room 4454. I'll call her to let her know that you all are on your way up.

Mrs. Dooley: Good, and thank you.

(Diamerald and Hanna decide to remain downstairs with Little Jay, Mark, and an officer while Mrs. Dooley and Kellie are escorted upstairs by another officer . . . Three minutes later, Mrs. Dooley, Kellie, and the officer exits the elevator and heads to Dr. Zanettoe's office. Dr. Zanettoe's secretary greets them as they enter)

Secretary: Hello, good evening, and how may I help you all?

Mrs. Dooley: Good evening; we are here to see Dr. Zanettoe.

Secretary: (while strolling down a list of names in front of her) Oh yes, Mrs. Dooley . . . Dr. Zanettoe is expecting you. Please, go right on in.

Mrs. Dooley: Thank you.

(Mrs. Dooley and Kellie enters Dr. Zanettoe's office. Dr. Zanettoe walks over to greet them with a hand shake, while introducing herslf. Then she points to the chairs in front of her desk and invites them both to have a seat . . .)

Dr. Zanettoe: So who do we have here? (Mrs. Dooley introduces herself and her sister, Kellie.) Oh, so you're Mrs. Dooley and she's your sister, Kellie? Well, let me begin by letting you two know that it's my pleasure to have this opportunity to meet with you all. Dr. Shaderi has told me about your tenacity and audacious faith.

Mrs. Dooley: Ooo..kay, so now what? Are we to commend you for that comment or dissociate ourselves?

Dr. Zanettoe: No, Mrs.Dooley! By no means would I want you all to do that. As a matter of fact, I am a big fan of anyone who believes in a higher power.

Kellie: Well, sorry to burst your bubble, Dr. Zanettoe, but we don't only believe that God is a higher power, because He's more than that to us; He's the ultimate power. He's our Lord and Saviour, Jehovah Jirah, our provider, Jehovah Ropheka, our healer, Jehovah Hoseenu, our maker, and Jehovah Elohim, our creator. With all that being said, who wouldn't want to trust in him, Dr. Zanettoe? Besides, He is the author and finisher of our faith.

Dr. Zanettoe: Alright, Kellie, settle down; I didn't mean to offend anyone. For I am a believer, too, and I know that God is not the author of confusion, but He is also Jehovah Shalom, our peace, so let's keep some of that in here. (They all laugh.)

Mrs. Dooley: Yeah, Kellie, I concur with Dr. Zanettoe, because you were getting kind of irate. I thought you were going to cuss the woman out for a second there, girl.

Kellie: Now Lillian, you know better than that! I admit, I do get agitated when someone limits God as if He is a mere, mortal man, because we all know good and well that He isn't.

Mrs. Dooley: Yes, I know, but lest you forget, Kellie, God doesn't need anyone to fight His battles; for He's God all by Himself.

Dr. Zanettoe: Excuse me, ladies . . . As much as I am enjoying this bible lesson, I beleive that we have some more pressing issues to resolve here. Wouldn't you all agree?

Mrs. Dooley: Oh, our bad, as the young people say. Please forgive us, Dr. Zanettoe; we have a tendancy to get carried away when it comes to discussing God's word.

Dr. Zanettoe: Oh, that's okay, I understand; no apology is necessary. Now about your husband, Mrs. Dooley, Dr. Shaderi gave me the impression that you all would like to consider the possibility of a euphenics operation.

Mrs. Dooley: I would say yes to that statement, Dr. Zanettoe, except I don't have the faintest idea of what you are talking about when you say "euphenics operation".

Dr. Zanettoe: Well, then I guess that was my bad, I'm sorry. I thought that Dr. Shaderi might've mentioned the subject, but seeing that he didn't, the term euphenics is defined as a movement in which one seeks to improve the human species by modifying an individual's biological developement, as through prenatal gene manipulation with chemicals.

Mrs. Dooley: I'm just as lost now than before you began to explain, Dr. Zanettoe. Can you try putting that in lame man's terms for us, please?

Dr. Zanettoe: Okay, let's see now . . . Are you all familiar with an old television show, from back in the early seventies, about an astronaut that was hurt very badly in a shuttle explosion?

Mrs. Dooley and Kellie: (simultaneously) Yes, that was the "Six Million Dollar Man".

Dr. Zanettoe: Okay. Well, that's sort of how your husband's reconstruction will be, Mrs. Dooley, only better.

Mrs. Dooley: Better?! How could you construct someone better than that guy, Dr. Zanettoe? I thought that that show was only science fiction.

Dr. Zanettoe: Exactly, Mrs. Dooley. However, we are living in a new age where just about everything is possible . . . Don't tell me that you are going against your own principals now. Just a few minutes ago, your sister, Kellie, here said that she didn't like it when people limited God, didn't she?

Kellie: Yeah, I said it, and I meant just that. So what about it, Dr. Zanettoe?

Dr. Zanettoe: Okay, then why do you think that the technology and capability of such a task would be science fiction in this day and time? Aren't you all familiar with the passage of scripture about the people in Babylon building the tower to heaven, wherein God Himself said that the people had become as one, meaning in unity? And the bible also says that where there is unity, there is strength to do whatever we put our minds to do. Why? All because this knowledge that we have comes from God. Now can I get an Amen, people?

Kellie: No, you can not get an Amen, Dr. Zanettoe, because you are picking parts of the scriptures to justify the means and not the end. You see, the knowledge in which you are referring to came from Adam and Eve eating of the fruit from the forbidden tree, the tree of knowledge of good and evil. The bible declares that, by doing so, they had become as gods, knowing good and evil. What I'm saying here, Dr. Zanettoe, is that although all that knowledge that you are referring to comes from God, that doesn't necessarily mean that it is being used properly.

Dr. Zanettoe: Okay, Kellie, I get your point. And not to get in a scriptural debate here, but isn't that what you two were doing when you quoted, "He who lives by the sword should die by the sword", and when your sister here, Mrs. Dooley, said that "One who does not take care of his household is worse than an infidel"?

I mean, excuse me if I'm wrong for saying so, but aren't we all doing the same thing here Kellie? Manipulating scriptures for our own means?

Mrs.Dooley: Kellie, I think you should hold up the white flag and surrender, because it looks like you have finally met your match, dear.

(They all laugh, and Kellie does surrender. Dr. Zanettoe is now about to finish explaining the euphenics precedure . . .)

Dr. Zanettoe: Okay, now that the religious aspect of this conversation has been addressed, shall we move on to the medical aspect?

Mrs. Dooley: Yes, by all means.

Dr. Zanettoe: Alright, now what I would like to propose here is that I call a very dear friend of mine, who I believe can be of great help to us. He is a self-made billionaire who specializes in physiognomic robotics and bionetrics. He was born in Russia but is now a U.S. citizen, and he has been wanting to further his developement in the field of bionetic robotics for quite some time now, so this would be a great opportunity for him to come aboard.

Mrs. Dooley: Hold on a minute, Dr. Zanettoe, what's with all this talk about robots? If you're talking about turning my husband into some sort of mechanical being, then I'm going to have to decline on participation. I don't think he would like that too well, and neither do I.

Dr. Zanettoe: Mrs. Dooley, I understand what you are saying and how you might feel. However, if your husband is to have a fighting chance at survival, you do not have much of a choice in the matter. Besides, we don't have a lot of timeto waste here, so I would encourage you to make a decision on this issue within the next couple of hours, or I'm afraid that Mr. Dooley won't be around for us to consider the matter at all. Now I don't mean to be mean spirited about the situation, but it is what it is. And with that being said, I must get back on my job right away if this task is to move forward. While I do so, maybe you should talk things over with your family, Mrs. Dooley . . . But again, keep in mind that time is of the essence, okay?

(Everyone say their goodbyes. Then Mrs. Dooley, Kellie, and the officer head back downstairs, where Diamerald, Little Jay, and Mark are. Little Jay, Mark, and Diamerald all run up to Mrs. Dooley and inquire what Dr. Zanettoe said. Mrs. Dooley asks everyone to follow her into the lounge and to have a seat while she explains what is on the table in terms of saving Mr. Dooley's life. Just as she begins to speak, her brother-in-law, Shawn, comes in along with Sergeant Willansby, Barbara, and Major Stephens . . .)

Mrs. Dooley: Well, as we all know, Jonathan was beaten pretty badly, so badly that his chance of survival doesn't look too promising.

(Little Jay starts to cry as his mom expresses his dad's condition and prognosis, so Diamerald cradles him in her arms to comfort him in his emotionality. Then Mrs. Dooley continues . . .)

Mrs. Dooley: However, after talking with the head physician here at the hospital, there seems to be one alternative in this matter, other than letting my husband die, and that is to reconstruct him as . . .

(Pauses as if she is about to cry, but doesn't. Instead, she continues on) . . . Okay, people, they want to do to Jonathan what they've done to Alofus.

(Everyone starts to murmur under their breaths, but Kellie quickly interrupts them . . .)

Kellie: Okay now people, time is of the essence, and a decision has to be made promptly and expeditiously. Therefore, we can not afford to waste time arguing or debating this issue. The meeting was only called to inform everyone of what's at hand. All we can do now is pray, and we need to do that now more than ever.

(After Kellie finishes talking, the meeting is adjourned, and Mrs. Dooley, Kellie, and the other officer goes back to Dr. Zanettoe's office to finalize the go ahead. Professor Greer and Dr. Kyzar are now both coming into the hospital. Diamerald greets them as they walk through the doors . . .)

Diamerald: Hello there, Professor Greer and Dr. Kyzar, good to see that you all made it; and just in the nick of time, because mom and Aunt Kellie just headed back upstairs to finalize my dad's situation.

Prof. Greer: Okay, Diamerald, and thanks for informing us of the situation. I guess we need to hurry on to meet with them, then. Can you tell me where we need to go?

Diamerald: Yeah, sure, Professor Greer; they are on the fourth floor of the south wing, room 4454. Ask for a Dr. Zanettoe.

Prof. Greer: Alright, thanks again. See you all later, okay dear?

(Shortly thereafter, Professor Greer and Dr. Kyzar both arrive on the fouth floor. They are greeted by the receptionist, who tells them to go right on in, so they are now entering Dr. Zanettoe's office.) (Mrs. Dooley properly introduces Professor Greer and Dr. Kyzar to Dr. Zanettoe, who is now speaking . . .)

Dr. Zanettoe: (while shaking their hands) Well, hello there, Professor Greer and Dr. Kyzar, how are you all doing? It's nice to finally meet you all. (Now looking at Professor Greer) I've been hearing about the great work that you and your associate, Dr. Elenski, have been doing over at the university.

Prof. Greer: First off, let me correct you, Dr. Zanettoe; Dr. Elenski and I are not associates, because he no longer works for the university. Secondly, I had nothing to do with this great work that you are alluding to; that was strictly Dr. Elenski, all by his lonesome self.

Dr.Zanettoe: Oh, I'm sorry, Professor, I didn't know that he was no longer employed with you all. And even if you really were involved with that new revolution in recreation, I wouldn't fault you. I mean, I don't think that anything is wrong with it because, personally, I am in favor of his theory.

Prof. Greer: Really, Dr. Zanettoe?! You're in favor of reinventing the human body?! . . . Well, it's quite alright if you choose to believe in Dr. Elenski's theories; I just needed to set the record straight that I had no part in his diabolical schemes.

Dr.Zanettoe: So you think that Dr. Elenski's actions were diablerie, Professor Greer?

Prof. Greer: Yes, without a doubt. Anytime an individual creates something for selfish gain, which hurts others . . . let's not forget to add that to the equation . . . then yes, it is by all means cruel and mischievous.

Kellie: I agree because this guy has done a lot of harm and damage to innocent people. Besides, his invention is a vexation of the spirit and is against what God created.

Dr.Zanettoe: Alright, I'm sorry folks, but although this debate about our friend, Dr. Elenski, is very interesting, I'm going to have to put a stop to it. We must move along with the situation surrounding Lieutenant Dooley. Now that being said, Mrs. Dooley, as I made mention to you all earlier, Dr. Gregory Breshkovsky is a dear friend of mine who is a Russian, born in the Ukraine. And he's a self made billionaire physiognomical roboticist scientist who now practices his research and lives here in the United States. Anyhow, he and a colleage of his are on their way over as we speak, to see if we can actually move this project forward. So until they arrive, I'd like for us to try and find some common grounds here in the matter regarding Lieutenant Dooley.

Mrs.Dooley: Good, that sounds just fine to me. I'm ready to get this thing moving because the sooner we start, the better the chances are for me to hold my husband again . . . even if he is half man, half robot. I'd rather have that than nothing at all.

Kellie: Yeah, I concur with my sister. I miss my brother-in-law dearly . . . even if he did get under my skin at times. He's a good guy, people, so if you all can get half of him back, we'll take it.

(Everybody laughs.)

Prof. Greer: Of course, we will do everything in our power to revitalize Mr. Dooley. Though I've only known him briefly, I've come to like him; he's a swell guy.

Dr. Kyzar: Yes, and I concur with my friend, Professor Greer here. Mr. Dooley and the entire family has moved me with much compassion as if they were my own family. And I wouldn't want anything less than to see them reunited.

(Meanwhile, back downstairs, Little Jay, Barbara, Diamerald, Hanna, and Mark are discussing Mr. Dooley's operation. Little Jay is now speaking . . .)

Little Jay: Diamerald, is dad going to be a robot when they finish operating on him?

Diamerald: Why, no he isn't, you knuckle head! And where on earth did you get such a notion?!

Little Jay: I got it from your knuckle headed room mate, that's where.

Diamerald: (Turns and looks at Hanna. Hanna looks away from her.) Hanna, did you just tell Little Jay that our dad would be a robot?

Hanna: Well, not exactly, D.A.

Diamerald: Well, what exactly did you tell him then, Hanna?

Hanna: Only that Mr. Dooley would be like the women in that movie "The Stepford wives", but I didn't mean anything by it. I was merely expressing my point of view on how the outcome might be, that's all, D.A.

(Over hearing their conversation, Barbara decides to voice her opinion of the matter.)

Barbara: Personally, I don't think that you should be expressing your point of view to a little boy who obviously is already upset over the fact that his dad is hurt. I don't think being told that his dad will be anything less than normal gives him much hope, do you? . . . Oh, my bad, that's just it . . . you weren't thinking, were you?

(Hanna is now very angry. She aggressively turns to Barbara, commences to walk toward her, raises her index finger and wiggles it, and bobs her head from side to side while saying . . .)

Hanna: Now I can see why Diamerald doesn't want you to be her sister, because you're a . . .

(Hanna is interrupted by Diamerald as Diamerald grabs her, puts her hand over her mouth, and asks her to be quiet. Now in awe, Little Jay and Mark look at them and wonder what in the world Hanna is talking about. Barbara is now responding to Hanna's statement . . .)

Barbara: (while smiling and focusing her attention now on Diamerald) Well, like it or not, baby sister, it is what it is.

(The tables turn, for Diamerald now has gotten very upset. She impulsively lets go of Hanna's mouth, turns toward Barbara, and slowly starts walking toward her with anger and rage in her eyes. With both of her hands cuffed into fists, Diamerald plunges at Barbara. And now Hanna tries to hold her back while begging her to stop. By this time, Sergeant Willansby, Major Stephens, and Shawn are walking down the hall, on their way in the room. Barbara has taken a defensive stance, one of the ready molds of defense that she had trained for in her karate class. Sergeant Willansby, Major Stephens, and Shawn have now walked in on all the commotion.

Sergeant Willansby is about to speak to her daughter, Barbara . . .)

Serg. Willansby: Barbara! What on earth is going on here?

Barbara: Well, to be honest, mom, I was just about to put a spanking on this big mouthed little girl here . . . Good thing you all showed up when you did, or I might've been going to jail today for assault.

(Diamerald plunges toward Barbara again. Fortunately, her uncle, Shawn, grabs her this time and asks her to settle down. However, Hanna too is now trying to get at Barbara because she was fueled by her statement as well. Major Stephens grabs her while Sergeant Willansby stands between her and Barbara. Meanwhile,

Little Jay and Mark are standing by, instigating and yelling, "Get her!" referring to Diamerald and Hanna getting Barbara. Shawn is now speaking to Diamerald . . .)

Shawn: Diamerald, why are you girls fueding, especially in a public facility?!

Diamerald: To be honest, Uncle Shawn, she started it and I was about to finish it. Luckily, you all came along when you did 'cause she was about to get a beat down (pointing at Barbara).

(After hearing Diamerald's statement, Barbara yells, "Well, bring it on, sister!")

Little Jay: You see now, Barbara? That's what got all this started in the first place. And why do you keep calling my sister "sister" anyway? What's up with that?

Barbara: (Replies angrily). What's up with it, Did you say what's up with it little boy?! Well I'll tell you what's up. What's up is that . . .

Sergt. Willansby: (Interrupts Barbara) Well, Little Jay, the reason my daughter keeps calling Diamerald sister is because they are both African American females and ahh . . . Yeah that's it; she meant no harm. (Turns to Barbara and asks her to apologize to them and to let them know that she meant no harm.)

Barbara: Yeah, my mom is right; I am sorry and I didn't mean any harm. I was just pointing out that she and I both are black females here from the mother land, Africa. And even though we have different fathers . . . some of us that is (looking at Diamerald with a smerk and being sarcastic) . . . that doesn't mean that we can't get along.

Maj. Stephens: I don't know what's going on here but whatever it is, I expect it to end this instant. (Looks at Hanna, Barbara, and Diamerald) Is that understood, young ladies?

(They all reply simultaneously, "Yes ma'am." So the ordeal surrounding Barbara and Diamerald ceases . . . for now. Meanwhile, back upstairs in Dr. Zanettoe's office, Dr. Breshkovsky and his colleague has arrived and are now being abreast of Mr. Dooley's situation. Dr. Zanettoe is now introducing everyone . . .)

Dr. Zanettoe: Mrs. Dooley, Kellie, Professor Greer, and Dr. Kyzar, I'd like to introduce you all to two very dear and wonderful friends of mine:(While pointing to) Dr. Gregory Breshkovsky and his colleague, Dr. Patricia Kukacovia. I met them both about ten years ago, in 1991, when I visited Moscow during an international medical convention.

(Everyone walks around and shakes hands, aquainting themselves with each other. Dr.Kyzar is now speaking to Dr. Kukacovia . . .)

Dr. Kyzar: So Dr. Kukacovia, we were told that Dr. Breshkovsky is from the Ukraine. Exactly what part of Russia are you from, may I ask? And what type of medicine do you practice?

Dr. Kukacovia: Well, my friend, I am from Moscow and I am a skin specialist. You see, I specialize in the tissues of the human body.

Dr. Kyzar: So I gather that you are a plastic surgeon, then?

Dr. Kukacovia: Yeah more or less. (They all laugh.)

Prof. Greer: Now what I'm curious to know from you, Dr. Breshkovsky, is what exactly are you proposing to do with the patient in question here? And how do you plan on bringing this operation into fruition financially? More importantly, how will you get past the political ramifications of such a task?

Mrs. Dooley: I'm glad you asked that question, Professor Greer, because it was heavy on my mind; I just didn't know whether or not it was feasible or proper for me to ask. However, now that those questions have been presented here, I'm anxious to hear your response, Dr. Breshkovsky.

Dr. Breshkovsky: First off, there's no need to despair about the financial aspect of this operation, so you all can let your minds be at ease. For I am fully prepared to fund the entire operation, from start to finish, with my own personal finances. Now that being said, let's move along to the political ramifications; I've already spoken to another personal and dear friend of mine and Dr. Zanettoe's, who just happens to be a United States senator and the president's right hand man. Therefore, we had no problem getting this operation under way.

Mrs. Dooley: Excuse me, Dr. Breshkovsky, but did I hear you correctly? Did you say that the operation has already commenced, sir?

Dr. Breshkovsky: That is precise, Madam Dooley. As a matter of fact, your husband, Master Dooley, is being prepped for surgery as we speak.

Kellie: Really?! Is he serious, Dr. Zanettoe? Can things move that fast?

Dr. Zanettoe: Yes, he is very serious. You all would be surprised to know how fast you can get things moving when you know the right people. And having a lot of money doesn't hurt either. If you all get my drift. (Everyone laughs.)

Mrs. Dooley: Well, don't mind me 'cause I ain't mad at you or Dr. Breshkovsky. You all go right ahead and use what he got and who he knows.

Kellie: And don't you forget who we know, sis. God works in mysterious ways, which is why I believe things are moving for us the way they are.

Prof. Greer: I'd say; wouldn't you, Dr. Kyzar?

Dr. Kyzar: Most certainly.

Dr. Zanettoe: Alright, good, looks like everything is in place and moving right along. So if you all don't mind, people, let's all do the same and move on to our designated locations. Mrs. Dooley and Kellie, I guess I'll be seeing you all a while later but for now, we all must be on our way to get prepped for surgery, okay?

Mrs. Dooley: Sounds good to me . . . Okay, Kellie, let's get out of here.

(Everyone says their good byes and Mrs. Dooley, Kellie and the officer all head back downstairs, where the rest of the crew is. Meanwhile, Dr. Zanettoe, Dr. Breshkovsky, Dr. Kyzar, and Professor Greer are all on their way to surgery.)

(Mrs. Dooley arrives back downstairs and is greeted by Little Jay, who eagerly runs up to her to tell her about the incident between Diamerald, Hanna, and Barbara. Knowingly, Shawn interrupts him and pulls him and Mark aside to warn them not to mention Diamerald, Hanna, and Barbara's altercation. They both comply. Major Stephens has gotten a call from Officer Cheryl Lansing, and is now answering . . .)

Maj. Stephens: Hello, Major Stephens here.

Ofc. Lansing: Hello, Major Stephens, ma'am, this is Officer Lansing. I'm calling to inform you that we have a possible break in the case of the Walsh's accident.

Maj. Stephens: Please excuse my ignorance, Officer Lansing, but if you don't mind, could you refresh my memory on that particular case? I seem to have gotten lost in this ordeal with Lieutenant Dooley.

Ofc. Lansing: Yes, of course. Well, two elderly individuals, Lieutenant Dooley's in-laws, were riding with their dog during that horrific rain storm we had about a year ago, ma'am, and were allegedly killed in a car wreck.

Maj. Stephens: Oh yes, now I remember . . . Okay, so what makes you feel that you have a break in the case, Officer Lansing?

Ofc. Lansing: Well, ma'am, we have a guy down here at the station who claims to have been on the scene when the accident occured.

Maj. Stephens: Really?! And he just decided to come forth a year later? Who is this guy, Officer Lansing? What's his name and what does he do for a living?

Ofc. Lansing: He says that his name is Glen Arthur, and he is obviously not doing anything to make a living right now. He claims to be a homeless, impecunious individual. He also said that he lives under the I-220 bridge corridor, where the Walsh's lost their lives. If he really lives there, then there may well be some validity to his story and knowledge of the case, ma'am.

Maj. Stephens: Alright then, Officer Lansing, hold this guy there and don't let him out of your sight. I'll be right there to question him personally.

Ofc. Lansing: Yes ma'am, will do.

(As Major Stephens hangs up, she informs Sergeant Willansby of the potential witness to the Walsh's deaths. Sergeant Willansby is also curious about this case because she has some personal interest in the matter. For she knew the victims, who were the parents of Mrs. Dooley and her sister, Kellie, but she won't dare tell them until they get concrete evidence in the matter. So Major Stephens and Sergeant Willansby both head down to headquarters to question the guy.)

(Major Stephens and Sergeant Willansby have arrived back at the station. They are in the interrogation room with the potential witness of the Walsh's car wreck, Glen Arthur. Major Stephens has placed an active tape recorder directly in front of the witness and is now questioning him . . .)

Maj. Stephens: So, for the record, sir, would you please tell us your name, where you live, and exactly what you witnessed on the night of March 8, 2010? And speak into the microphone.

(While leaning toward the recorder, Mr. Arthur begins to speak stammeringly. For he has a speech impediment unbeknown to Major Stephens and Sergeant Willansby . . .)

Mr. Arthur: My n-n-name is G-Glen A-Arthur, and I la-live undider th the t-two twenty b-bridge.

Maj. Stephens: (Realizing that Mr. Arthur has a speech impediment) Ok now, Mr. Arthur, just calm down and take your time.

Mr. Arthur: Ooo . . . k-kay, we-we-well, it wa-wa-was rai-rai-rainin' v-very h-hard the n-night of Ma-March e-eight, t-two thousand t-ten, an-and I wa-was ly-lyin' undider the b-bridge and I h-h-heard a v-v-very l-l-loud scree-scree-screechin' s-s-sound. And th-then, I h-heard a b-big b-boom s-s-sound, s-s-so I g-got up and ra-ran out t-to s-s-see wha-what had happened.

(Sergeant Willansby is getting very impatient as she listens to Mr. Arthur express himself, so she just decides to ask him to write the rest of the information down on paper. Major Stephens is also getting irritated by his speech impediment so she agrees with Sergeant Willansby's request. They give him a legal pad and step outside to converse in private. Sergeant Willansby is now speaking to Major Stephens . . .)

Serg. Willansby: (While both are laughing) Ma'am, if I would have stayed in there a couple more minutes, I would have been on my way to hell for laughing in that poor guy's face.

Maj. Stephens: (Still laughing) You too? I'm not sure if his testimoney would even be admissible, even if there is some validity to his story.

Serg. Willansby: And why is that, Major Stephens?

Maj. Stephens: Because he would probably be deemed as insignificant, and most people would probably prefer that he was reticent after hearing him try to communicate.

Serg. Willansby: Oh no, I'm not going to let that happen. As I told you, Major Stephens, this case is somewhat personal to me. You see, the Walsh's were Mrs. Dooley's and Kellie's parents and the in-laws of Lieutenant Dooley; not to mention, my daughter's grandparents . . .

(Sergeant Willansby blurted out that last statement by accident, and now realizes her blunder. Major Stephens was unaware of it until now, so she begins to question Sergeant Willansby . . .)

Maj. Stephens: So tell me, Sergeant Willansby, was that what all the commotion between your daughter, Barbara, and Lieutenant Dooley's daughter, Diamerald, was all about?

Serg. Willansby: Well, to be perfectly honest, Major Stephens, yes and if you gotta know . . . yes, my daughter is Lieutenant Dooley's daughter. So there you have it . . . Now you don't have to wonder or ask me any more questions, okay?

Maj. Stephens: (Is now embarrassed for Sergeant Willansby and ashamed herself for prying) I'm sorry, Sergeant Willansby, please forgive me for sticking my nose where it didn't belong.

Serg. Willansby: Oh, that's quite alright, Major Stephens. I'm tired of hiding my baby's and my life from everyone anyway. You see, this thing happened before Lieutenant Dooley married Mrs. Dooley, so I don't feel quite as embarrassed by it as you may think. With that being said, I'd like to just drop this subject altogether, if that's okay with you, ma'am.

Maj. Stephens: Yeah sure, I understand . . . And don't you worry, my lips are sealed.

(They both say good bye and part ways. Major Stephens heads to her office and Sergeant Willansby goes to meet up with Barbara for lunch . . .)

(Major Stephens is now in her office, awaiting Officer Lansing, who she has asked to join her. As Officer Lansing enters the door, Major Stephens points to a chair while saying . . .)

Maj. Stephens: Hello, Officer Lansing, please come right on in and have a seat . . . Now about this homeless character, why didn't you warn me of his speech impediment? I almost lost my mind trying to figure out what he was trying to convey to Sergeant Willansby and I.

Ofc. Lansing: Oh, I'm sorry ma'am, but I totally forgot after the chief ordered me to call the hospital and check up on Lieutenant Dooley's condition.

Maj. Stephens: To do what?! Now why on God's green earth would Chief McClemens be interested in Lieutenant Dooley's condition, especially when he doesn't even like the guy?

Ofc. Lansing: Yeah, my sentiments exactly, ma'am. It does make you wonder, doesn't it?

Maj.Stephens: No, not really. Actually, I sort of expected it. After all, how else would he know what his next move should be . . . if you get my drift.

Ofc. Lansing: I guess I do, but how could Lieutenant Dooley hamper any of the chief's actions when he's in the hospital in critical condition, ma'am?

Maj. Stephens: Is that the report that you gave him, Officer Lansing?

Ofc. Lansing: Well, I haven't told him anything yet, ma'am. As a matter of fact, he is waiting on me to get back to him right now.

Maj. Stephens: Good! Now here's what I want you to tell him . . . Tell him that the doctor said that the lieutenant is in a very critical condition and that his chances of pulling through are slim to none. Tell him that they are just waiting for the family to decide whether or not to pull the plug, because he's not breathing on his own.

Ofc. Lansing: Now why would I do that, Major Stephens?

Maj. Stephens: Because I'm ordering you to, Officer Lansing. And don't let him on that I asked you to do so, is that understood?

Ofc. Lansing: Yes ma'am; perfectly.

Maj. Stephens: Okay, good enough. Now get to it right away . . . And oh yeah, Officer Lansing . . .

Ofc. Lansing: Yes, Major Stephens?

Maj. Stephens: If you don't mind, keep the homeless guy as a secret to the chief as well, at least until I can make some sense of his story.

Ofc. Lansing: I got you, Major; Roger that.

(Officer Lansing exits Major Stephens' office . . . Major Stephens is now calling her spouse, Captain Joshua Stephens, who heads the Jackson Police Training Academy . . .)

Maj. Stephens: Hello, sweetheart, how are you doing?

Capt. Stephens: Oh, I'm doing just great, honey. What's up with you? Is everything alright? Are you okay?

Maj. Stephens: Yeah, I'm okay. Now why are you asking?

Capt. Stephens: Because I can distinguish your attitude by your tone of voice. Besides, you usually call me sweetheart when something is wrong or when you want something; all other times, it's Joshua.

Maj. Stephens: Oh, I do? Well I hadn't noticed, but since you've asked, yeah something is wrong. Do you remember when you told me that Sergeant Willansby seemed to be in a relationship with Lieutenant Dooley even though, at that time, she was involved with a guy named Raymond Byrd?

Capt. Stephens: Yeah, what about it?

Maj. Stephens: Well, it turns out you were right, and guess what . . . they had a baby together.

Capt. Stephens: Now Sharon, haven't I told you about gossiping and spreading rumors, honey? Now this baby that you are referring to, it wouldn't happen to be a female about the age of 21, would it?

Maj. Stephens: Yeah, but how on earth do you know that Joshua? Did you already know about this baby?

Capt. Stephens: No, but I did suspect it because right after the lieutenant requested a transfer, Sergeant Willansby ended up being pregnant, and she broke up with that Raymond character who I believe ended up dying of cancer shortly thereafter. Sergeant Willansby fiercely tried to get Lieutenant Dooley back but by then, another beautiful young lady named Lillian had his nose wide open. However, I personally don't believe that he ever got over Sergeant Willansby.

Maj. Stephens: You don't?! And why is that my darling hubbie who asked me not to go around gossiping, yet is here talking unstoppably about someone else's business?

(They both laugh.)

Capt. Stephens: Well, you got a point, so I'll just stop here before I be dubbed as a backbiting cop.

Maj. Stephens: No, honey, not now! . . . You gotta finish telling me why you don't think that he got over Sergeant Willansby. After that, you can be converted to a peace keeper.

Capt. Stephens: Well okay, but this is the last time. You see, it's because I saw the lieutenant with Sergeant Willansby on several different occasions, holding the child and playing with it as though they had a connection.

Maj. Stephens: Ah, is that it, Joshua? No wonder you didn't make homocide detective. I thought you had something juicy. Good bye, now go back to your training class. There's a lot more for everyone to learn, sweetie. (Major Stephens hangs up in her husband's face because she is dissappointed in his answer.)

(Sergeant Willansby has just drove up to the Poe Pemp's restaurant, where her daughter, Barbara, is already inside, waiting for her. Meanwhile, back at the hospital, Lieutenant Dooley is being operated on. Shawn has spoken to Mrs. Dooley and Kellie about going downtown to the police station to press charges against JPD for neglecting the safety of a prisoner in transport. He also told them that they should name Chief McClemens in the affidavit.

Now they are all headed to the police station. While en route, Shawn decides to call a dear friend of his, a black female by the name of Lois Macfield, who is a United States senator. The senator is now answering the phone on her private line . . .)

Sen. Macfield: Hello? Senator Macfield.

Shawn: Hello, Senator Macfield, how are you? This is Shawn Hogan.

Sen. Macfield: Oh, hi there, Shawn! I'm just great. It's been a while since I've heard from you, so please forgive me for not recognizing your voice. How are things with you? And please call me Lois.

Shawn: Well that's quite alright, Senator Macfield . . . I mean, Lois. I'm sorry, I've developed a habit of giving respect and honor to people who deserve it. Anyhow, to answer your question, Lois, I'm not doing too good right now,well not me personally. But a very dear friend of mine, has gotten himself into some serious trouble, which is why I'm phoning you.

Sen. Macfield: I'm sorry to hear that Shawn. What seems to be the problem? Hopefully, I can be of service to you. After all, I do owe you one. (They both laugh, and then Shawn responds . . .)

Shawn: Yeah, you do, don't you? I had forgotten about that.

Sen. Macfield: Yeah right! You forget a debt, Shawn? An elephant stands a better chance of forgetting.

Shawn: Oh, am I that demanding of recompense? I didn't know, but now that you've reminded me, let's see if I can cash in on some of that debt.

Sen. Macfield: Okay, come on with it because honestly, I don't like being indebted to anyone.

Shawn: Alright, now let's get serious here, Lois.

Sen. Macfield: I am. Did you think that I was kidding?

Shawn: No, I believe you Lois, but for real all jokes aside, I really do need your help on this one, Asap.

Sen. Macfield: Alright, what is it, Shawn?

Shawn: It's my brother-in-law. He's on the police force here in Jackson and he has managed to get himself in a pretty bad dilemma, Lois. He was arrested. But he never made it to the jail.

Sen. Macfield: This brother-in-law of yours, his name wouldn't happen to be Dooley, would it?

Shawn: As a matter of fact, it is, but how did you know?

Sen. Macfield: Shawn, I'm a senator who helps to get laws passed. It's my job to know what's going on with the law, especially local. Besides, the attorney general and I have been dating for six months now and he has been keeping me abreast of the local commotions. (They both laugh.)

Shawn: So what exactly has your companion told you about my brother-in-law, and please tell me your personal thoughts on the matter as well.

Sen. Macfield: Now Shawn, I'm sure you already know this but just to be certain that we are on the same page, you can't reveal me as the source of what I'm about to tell you, okay? . . . (Shawn agrees) . . . All the attorney general told me is that your brother-in-law, Mr. Dooley, well the reason he never made it to jail. Is because he has managed to step on the toes of some big-footed criminals, and he hopes that Mr. Dooley gets out of it alive. Personally, if he does make it out alive, I think that your brother-in-law should meet with my other friend, Govenor Hatchetson, because I believe she is the only one who's in a position to help him. Also Shawn, if he makes it out of the surgery that he is presently undergoing, please get back in touch with me Asap. Meanwhile, I'll put in a good word to the govenor, okay? Not to be rude, sweetie, but I must be going.

Shawn: Okay, I'll be sure to do just that; and thanks for everything, Lois.

(They both say good bye and hang up.)

(Meanwhile, Chief McClemens is in his office back at the Jackson Police Department. His mother, Mrs. Marsha McClemens Adovis, is now knocking at his door. After the chief invites her in, Mrs. Adovis enters and begins to speak . . . Mrs. Adovis is aware of her son Chief McClemens part in the death of the late Dr. Satcher. Both she and her son knew of Dr. Satcher being her late husbands bastard child, but they did not know that Dr. Elenski was his child, well lets just say that Chief McClemens didn,t know. For his mom always did suspicion that something was amiss with the late Sara Belford who was always sick and throwing up. But then after about nine months space she ironically got to feeling better after a mysterious trip away from their home for about a week, and then returns feeling much better . . . Of course this was the time Dr. Elenski,s mom left him on the porch of a friend of hers who could not bare children, but wanted to so badly. And this friend kept the child after reading a note asking her to take care of my baby as if it was yours. Supposing that God had mysteriously and miraculously sent her this child, so she reared the Lad until he was six years old. This is when little Mirac, named by his adopted mom Mrs. Lazariah Elenski, who was married to a Mr. Trerrell Elenski who since has passed away due to prostate cancer, and Mrs. Lazariah Elenski too had died of Lupus vulgaris. And they had no other living relatives here in the United States, for they had come over from Venezuella on a visa, and ended up becoming legal aliens once here for some time. Dr. Elenski had been given the name Mirac (which is short for miracle) Earl Elenski, But after running away and growing up, he had changed his middle name from Earl to Eveil . . . Go figure) . . . (Giving him the full name of Mirac Eveil Elenski).

Mrs. Adovis: (hastily walks in with a fierce look on her face) Junior! Just what on earth were you thinking when you ordered Lieutenant Dooley's arrest?!

Chief McClem: (has a fearful look on his face because up to this point since his child hood, he has been very intimidated by his mother) Well, I . . . I w-was hoping to scare him off the case, mom.

Mrs. Adovis: (yelling) Scare him?! Scare him?! Junior, ya'll practically beat the man to death, and you say that you only meant to scare him? My God, son, what would you have done if you were trying to kill him?

Chief McClem: Mom, please settle down and lower your voice. You are in the police chief's office, you know? And it doesn't look good with you coming in here yelling at me as if I'm still a kid or something.

Mrs. Adovis: To hell with what it looks like! And as for you being chief of police, that problem can easily be remedied. As a matter of fact, I'm considering your replacement as chief. (Mrs. Adovis' husband is Jackson's mayor and he has the power to hire or fire the chief of police.)

Chief McClem: (with a look of despair) You wouldn't dare, mom! It wasn't my fault. Your pal, Dr. Elenski is the one who ordered that monster he created to rough the lieutenant up. They're the ones who went overboard, so if you want to take your rage out on someone, try blaming my late little brother Dr. Satcher and your late ex husband's son who fired the poor guy from his job and pissed him off. (Chief McClemens still not knowing that Dr. Elenski is also his half brother, nor is he (Dr. Elenski) aware of the Chief or Dr. Satcher being his brother . . . Mrs. Adovis and Dr. Elenski had gotten acquainted at a fund raising function a couple years back. Again Dr. Elenski not knowing that she was the widow of his late dad Joesph McClemens or even knowing who his real dad or mom was even).

(Mrs. Adovis' entire demeanor has drastically changed and now her spirit is exceptionally low.)

Mrs. Adovis: Why? Why would you bring up such a distasteful event, Junior? Don't you think I've been hurt enough?

Chief McClem: I'm sorry mom, I didn't want to bring it up but you gave me no choice, threatening to fire me for something that, that bastard child you allowed your husband to bring into this world had done.

Mrs. Adovis: (yelling hysterically again) Me?! I had nothing to do with your dad's extramarital affairs, Junior! It was said that Dr. Satcher was the son of another guy who Sarah was alledgedly dating at the time. But obviously, I knew that was a lie when the baby started to grow and take shape (Now yelling even more angrily and louder) and began to look more like Joesph each day!

(Mrs. Adovis begins to wrench a scarf in her hands as if imaginatively strangling something or someone. Chief McClemens comes over and puts his arms around her to console her. Then he commences to speak to her . . .)

Chief McClem: Mom, it's okay. It's alright now, mom. We will recompense this city for all the hurt and embarassment that it has put us through, I promised myself every since I was nine years old that I would never again let anyone hurt you and get away with it. Now you just go on back home and let me handle things; I got a plan that will even rid us of Dr. Elenski soon.

Mrs. Adovis: (With a look of fear, because she knows how vindictive Dr. Elenski can be.) A what?! Did you say you had a plan to get rid of Dr. Elenski? Are you insane, Junior, or are you just tired of living? Do you know what you are saying? I hope you haven't mentioned this to anybody else.

Chief McClem: Now why do you think I'm insane, mom? Is it because I'm not afraid of this character like you and your free loading husband are? Well, I'm sorry, I'm not about to bow down to him. And when I get through with him, you all will look to me as the man, just you wait and see.

Mrs. Adovis: Junior, please son, you're the only one I got left to remember your father by. I don't want you to get yourself killed. That guy, Dr. Elenski, is a lot like your dad was. He will stop at nothing to get what he wants, and to be perfectly honest, son, you are a lot like your mommy. You're just mouth and, unfortunately, you really don't have a heart for killing.

Chief McClem: Really?! Well, who do you think got rid of that no good husband of yours and his mistress, huh mom? And why would you want to remember that creator of bastards?

(A sudden, eery silence immediately fills the room. Mrs. Adovis is now looking at her son, Chief McClemens, with a look of fear and unbelief as he stares back with a smerk and an evil, sinister look that she has never seen before . . . The scene of events are begining to change drastically, Chief McClemens and Dr. Elenski are about to commence battling with each other not realizing that they are half brothers and also brothers to the late Dr. Satcher).

(Meanwhile, back at the Poe Pemp's restaurant, Sergeant Willansby and her daughter, Barbara are waiting for the waitress to bring out their food. While waiting, they are discussing the situation surrounding Lieutenant Dooley's health and the matter about him being Barbara's dad . . . Barbara is now speaking to her mom, Sergeant Willansby.)

Barbara: They need to hurry up and bring out that food because I'm so famished, I don't think a leg of lamb will suffice; I might just eat the entire lamb.

Sergt. Williansby: You?! Girl, I'm so hungry that . . . well, you know how I like to bite off my nails when I'm nervous? . . . Well, let's just say I forgot to spit them out.

Barbara: Ewe, that's nasty! TMIG!

Sergt. Willansby: TMIG? What in the heck does that mean?

Barbara: It means that you are nasty, mom and that you're giving me too much information. Some things are meant to be kept to yourself.

Sergt. Willansby: My darling daughter, I know you're not talking about keeping things to ourselves. When I didn't tell you about a particular thing that I thought to keep to myself, you got pissed off . . . Now which is it, do I tell you or don't I?

Barbara: Now mom, you know that telling me who my dad was was entirely different from telling me something that would make me puke.

Sergt. Willansby: Oh, really now? Well, I can't see the difference because just as my nasty habit makes you want to puke, my pregnancy with you had me puking.

Barbara: At first, I just thought it mom, but now it's official: you're crazier than a bessie bug.

Sergt. Willansby: Why am I crazy, Barabara and tell me, what exactly is a bessie bug?

Barbara: Oh, you mean to tell me that you don't know? Well, all I can tell you is, I remember grandma saying something about it when I was younger.

Sergt. Willansby: No, I'm sorry darling, I can't seem to remember having a conversation with NaNa about a bessie bug . . . Oh yeah, it just came to me! . . . It was that night when you snuck out of the window, trying to get to that guy, Allen. I told your NaNa about it and she said that you were crazier than a bessie bug, but I knew she wasn't talking about a real bug. Of course we all know that it's this Pepsi generation that takes things literally.

Barbara: Oh, no you did'ent go there, mom! Just a few minutes ago, you were probably going through your brain, trying to figure out what TMIG spelled, not realizing it was an acronym.

(Sergt. Willansby and Barbara are now both laughing, as the waitress appears with their meal. Barbara decides to comment on the lengthy time it took to get their food.)

Barbara: So how's the weather in Africa these days? (They all laugh. Sergeant Willansby decides to respond in defense of the waitress.)

Sergt. Willansby: Oh, don't pay her no mind, child; even her NaNa said that she was crazier than a bessie bug.

(When they all stop laughing, the waitress leans over to ask Sergeant Willansby a question.)

Waitress: I don't want to seem stupid or anything but what exactly is a bessie bug?

(Sergt. Willansby and Barbara both look at each other and laugh even harder. This offends the waitress, who replies, "Looks like both of you are crazier than that bug" and then turns and walks off hastily.)

(Sergeant Willansby and Barbara are almost done eating and are about to discuss a more sensitive issue, the possibility of divulging the secret that Lieutenant Dooley is Barbara's biological father. While reaching over to grab her daughters hands, Sergeant Willansby begins speaking . . .)

Sergt. Willansby: Barbara, my darling sweet heart, I'd just like to begin by telling you how sorry I am for causing you to miss out on some of the best years of your life, and for hindering you from getting acquainted and having a relationship with one of the most important men of your life. I'd also like to say that, even though you and Diamerald don't seem to get along, I saw the connection between you two. I should've let the truth run its course, because God even says that the truth will set you free in his Word, free from the hurt and anguish that you have had to endure for all these years. Barbara dear, I'm so very sorry; please forgive me for my selfish act.

(Sergeant Willansby begins to cry and drops her head in remorse. At that very moment, Barbara grips her mom's hands even tighter, as her eyes begin to fill with tears as well. She begins to respond to her mom's apology . . .)

Barbara: Mom . . . please look at me. Hear me and hear me well. You shouldn't beat up on yourself as if it's solely your fault, because Lieutenant Dooley and society equally share the blame in this ordeal. Irregardless of whose to blame, it's a done deal. I'm here and I'm healthy, we both are, and that's what matters right now, so please let it go, mom and let's move on with our lives as God would want us to. Remember what the scripture declares, he who looks back is not fit to enter into the kingdom.

Sergt. Willansby: (gets up and walks around the table to give her daughter a big hug) Sweet heart, I am so proud to have you as my daughter and I wouldn't trade you for the world. If I had to do it all over again, the only thing I'd change is that I would marry Lieutenant Dooley.

Barbara: Now mom, why would you say such a thing? If you would've married Lieutenant Dooley, the present Mrs. Dooley would not have married him and Diamerald and Little Jay would not have been born. That would leave me without my siblings, and to be honest, I'm kind of feeling this big sister thing. (They both laugh.)

Sergt. Willansby: Well, who's to say that I would not have borne you
some siblings? Their names may not have been Diamerald and
Little Jay but you would've had siblings. (They both laugh
again. As they're laughing, Sergeant Willansby gets a call from
Major Stephens . . .)

"Man's Best Friend" Vol. 2 (closing)
The solidarity of Alofus and Lieutenant Dooley on the horizon

This is not the end, but the beginning of many things to come from this new Author John A. Greer Sr., who would like to thank all who supported him by purchasing and reading his first edition of vol.1 "Man's Best Friend' and for purchasing this copy as well of "Man's Best Friend' Vol.2 Entitled: "The Solidarity Of Alofus And Lieutenant Dooley On The Horizon" and asked that you all stay tuned tuned for vol. 3 of " Man's Best Friend" Entitled:" The Show Down"of the first edition coming soon to a book store near you. And in closing he would like to leave these proverbs with you the readers... [To Always Remember.]

"When choosing a book to read"

Choose one that you can understand, one that carries the D-scarf syndrome.

"A great patriarch once said, 'In all thy getting, get an understanding'

And that's exactly what one would be getting when reading books with the D-scarf syndrome in mind.

By John A. Greer Sr.

An excerpt from the coming Volume 3 of the first Edition of
"Man's Best Friend"
(But the Entire City Loves Him)
"The Show Down"

In Volume 3 which is the final chapter of the first edition of "Man's Best Friend" (But the Entire City Loves Him). Lieutenant Dooley and Alofus (the dog) both are about to come out of recovery from their injuries inflicted upon them by that sinister villain in the story named Money Mike. They will be uniting together as fighting partners in crime now that they both have been converted into bionic form. And of course they will be seeking to avenge the culprits who harmed them. Also, it will be interesting to find out how Mrs. Dooley will handle it when she finds out that her husband Lieutenant Dooley and his former partner Sergeant Williansby has a child together. Now will Lieutenant Dooley's new bionic form be able to withstand the beat down that's about to befall him from his angry spouse. To find out the conclusion of this matter and the circumstances surrounding Alofus Lieutenant Dooley and Money Mike, stay tuned and look for the Volume 3 final edition of the first edition of "Man's Best Friend" (But the Entire City Loves Him). Entitled *"The Show Down"* coming soon to your favorite bookstores.

By John A. Greer Sr.

ALOFUS

ALOFUS CATCHING
FRISBEE THROWN BY
LITTLE JAY